Percival David Foundation
of Chinese Art

A Guide to the Collection

Percival David Foundation of Chinese Art

A Guide to the Collection

Rosemary E. Scott
Curator

With an Introduction by Lady David

Percival David Foundation of Chinese Art
School of Oriental and African Studies
University of London

Published by the School of Oriental and African Studies,
University of London
© Percival David Foundation of Chinese Art 1989

ISBN 0 7286 0150 8

Designed by Rosanne Chan and Sze-fung Chan
Colour separation by Goody Color Separation (Scanner) Ltd.
Printed by C & C Offset Printing
Produced by Millennia Limited, Hong Kong

[handwritten note: Tele. 0207 3873909. weekdays. open. 10/5 etc.]

Contents

Acknowledgements

I would like to express my gratitude to all my colleagues at the
Percival David Foundation, especially to Glenn Ratcliffe who is
responsible for all the photographs in this volume, to Elizabeth
Jackson and Ming Wilson without whose invaluable effort and
forbearance the manuscript could not have been produced,
and to Jean Martin and Ann Marie Gerling for all their kindness
and help. I am grateful to Catherine Lawrence for the map of
kiln sites. I would also like to thank Martin Daly and Rose Kerr
for their advice and support, and Hin-cheung Lovell in Hong
Kong for undertaking all the production arrangements.

Rosemary E. Scott
Bloomsbury, 1988

Introduction by Lady David

Nature and Scope of the Collection

The Percival David Foundation of Chinese Art was opened on 10 June 1952 by the Chancellor of the University of London, the Earl of Athlone, accompanied by his wife, Her Royal Highness The Princess Alice. In his opening address, the Chancellor said:

> Two years ago, Sir Percival David made to the University his magnificent gift, the Collection of Chinese Ceramics and the Library of Chinese and Western books that he had built up over the course of twenty years with such care and taste. In return the University has provided a worthy home for these treasures. It is not often that we have the honour and the pleasure of the presence of the benefactor when the time comes for others to enjoy the fruits of his generosity; but I trust that Sir Percival may long be with us to aid us with his profound knowledge of Chinese art and to appreciate the enjoyment and stimulus which his gift will undoubtedly provide.

The Times of 6 June, commenting on this splendid acquisition, said:'The University of London has received many notable gifts since its foundation in 1836, but it has seldom received a benefaction of wider or more general interest than that recently bestowed upon it by Sir Percival David.'

Since 1952 the Collection has been installed in its quarters of a converted townhouse at Number 53, Gordon Square, a 19th century area of Bloomsbury (**1**). The Collection comprises some 1,400 items of Chinese ceramics of the Song, Yuan, Ming and Qing dynasties, that is, from the 10th to the 18th century. With a few exceptions Sir Percival limited himself to wares no earlier than the Song, so that he could assemble a collection of quality that would be of unique value to scholars and students.

Certainly in its superlative quality the Collection is unparalleled except by the former Imperial Collection, now in the National Palace Museum in Taibei. Indeed some pieces in the David Collection had been acquired from the former Imperial Collection. The Collection is also extremely rich in documentary pieces, having a higher percentage of marked and inscribed specimens than any other in the world, many of the inscriptions being documents of prime importance. A number of Song pieces are engraved with poems and comments composed by the Qing emperor Qianlong, expressing his admiration for them. Even more important are the specimens with inscriptions contemporary with their manufacture, for these throw light on many facets of Chinese culture. Assembled under ideal conditions by a connoisseur with a restlessly probing mind and keen aesthetic judgement, the Collection is an invaluable source of information on the art, history, philosophy, literature, and traditions of the Chinese people in a period spanning almost one thousand years.

The Library is of special interest, having many rare and some unique items in East Asian and Western languages, including periodicals and reference books. It is essentially a working library, designed to complement and document the Collection.

1 The Percival David Foundation at 53, Gordon Square, London WC1H 0PD.

History of the Collection
The 1920s and 1930s

Percival David was born in Bombay, India, in 1892, and succeeded to the title in 1926. Having graduated from the University of Bombay and Cambridge University, and attained a degree in law, he intended to pursue that subject as a career until Chinese art and archaeology took precedence and became his sphere of endeavour. It was to prove beyond any doubt the wisest decision he could have made, endowed as he was with a historical imagination that gave him an insight into the values and ways of thought of alien and ancient cultures. In addition he was a born collector, possessing great pertinacity and a retentive visual memory that enabled him to seize every opportunity to make important additions to his collection.

By 1924 Percival David had already acquired a considerable mastery of the Chinese written language, but at the time there were few opportunities in the West for a serious study of Chinese art. The few examples of Chinese art that had found their way to England had so captivated him that he decided to visit China itself. His aim was to study the tradition of art connoisseurship as it was practised in China, and that at the highest level of manifestation – the Imperial Collection.

This was then housed in the Forbidden City in Beijing (Peking), the treasures being stored in boxes or lying around haphazardly with little attention to display. Sir Percival was able to convince the palace officials that a more impressive display of some of their treasures might be arranged in one of the smaller pavilions, where they could be viewed by all Chinese citizens who had heard of them and been anxious for so long to see some examples of their ancient heritage. A building eminently suitable for the purpose was located, but required extensive restoration. Sir Percival offered to finance the project himself, to the great appreciation of all concerned. The exhibition was a tremendous success, a catalogue was published, and the attendance far surpassed all expectations.

Sir Percival returned to London in the following year, but went again to China in 1927. On this occasion rumours were circulating that prospective buyers were endeavouring to acquire some of the Imperial Collection which had been offered as collatoral to the Yuin Yeh Bank by the Dowager Empress, whose departure from the Forbidden City in 1901 had required substantial financial assistance.

According to reliable sources, two such overtures had been initiated, but in each case a serious threat had been made on the life of the prospective purchaser should he attempt to remove the objects from Beijing. Both considered the intimidation a bluff, but when the pressure persisted, each in turn retreated. With complete disregard for his own safety, Sir Percival decided to stake his bid for the objects; he was determined that nothing would stand between him and the success that had eluded his predecessors.

At this point it emerged that a high official of the Bank in question was also a collector and obviously wanted the treasures for himself. Whether he was the initiator of the threats will never be known. Through official contacts it was eventually arranged for Sir Percival to visit the Bank and see the treasures. They were magnificent, and as their beauty intensified in his eyes, so did his determination to acquire them. As a result of diligent pursuit and despite almost insuperable obstacles during months of negotiations, Sir Percival finally persuaded the assembled Board to accept his proposal. A selection of some forty pieces was made and the financial terms settled. The money was deposited, and the Bank was informed, only to have it repudiate the agreement and renege on the transaction! Desperately as Sir Percival wanted the treasures, his initial reaction was that of incredulity at the dishonourable behaviour of the Bank. Now, however, his position was to be reversed again by the intervention of the friendly Secretary, who advised Sir Percival to leave Beijing for Japan where he could find a respite from the very cold winter. He would thus distance himself from the tawdry affair. When negotiations could be renewed, the Secretary would cable, 'Lovely weather in Peking'.

This duly happened, and Sir Percival returned. The atmosphere at the Bank was now cordial, and the transaction would be consummated as originally planned. The chosen objects were divided by Sir Percival into three categories: the pieces of lesser quality were to be shipped first, to be followed by a second shipment, and the most precious pieces to be shipped last. Now came the problem of their removal from Beijing. For this intricate operation, a close personal Japanese friend and, incidentally, an art dealer, was chosen, because he regularly made the round trip to his homeland. After the first shipment had cleared customs at Seoul, the dealer telegraphed Sir Percival that 'brother was in good health'. The same procedure was adopted for the second shipment. The transmission of the final and most precious cargo appeared in jeopardy when the eagerly awaited telegram reached Sir Percival saying 'brother ill and in hospital'. This disturbing news was quickly followed by the arrival at his hotel of the dealer's wife and six small children, the distraught lady demanding, 'What have you done with my husband?' Three days later, the friend returned to relate the story of how he had celebrated with the customs officials the, as he thought, successful conclusion of his mission, only to awake the next morning in jail! A guard was bribed to summon a local dealer friend to the prison, who was fortunately able to secure the Japanese dealer's release. From Japan the treasures travelled across the United States, and are now displayed in all their glory at the Foundation.

Sir Percival journeyed home to London in 1929, but went back to China in 1930-1, where he again devoted himself to working with the palace officials in organizing other exhibitions, and in making a comprehensive inventory of the contents of the various halls and palaces. He was also able to acquire through dealers and other contacts many more fine pieces for his own collection.

The year 1931 was one of particular significance for it was then that I first met Sir Percival. At that initial meeting Sir Percival showed me his fabulous collection of Chinese art treasures. I was entranced by its beauty, and he decided then and there to explain to

11

2 This photograph taken at the 1935-6 Exhibition shows Sir Percival David, two Japanese specialists, Lawrence Binyon, His Royal Highness The Crown Prince of Sweden, Professor Yukio Yashiro and Oscar Raphael with a bronze vessel from the Nezu Museum.

me the various nuances of the subject. After putting me through a gruelling test which I seem to have passed with honours, he assigned me a solo two-hour session with the Collection, during which I had to select the twelve most important items. This test I also passed with a perfect score; thereupon Sir Percival became so impressed with my keen appreciation and developing knowledge of the subject that he appointed me Curator of his Collection. Later I became his wife.

The year 1931 also saw the opening of the Dorchester Hotel in Park Lane, where Sir Percival's Collection, having outgrown its smaller accommodation in the Mayfair Hotel, was duly installed. It remained there until the outbreak of the Second World War, when it was sent to Sir Percival's country home for safety.

It was also in 1931 that Sir Percival took the first step towards creating a programme of study of Chinese art. He established a Chair of Chinese Art and Archaeology at the Courtauld Institute, an institute affiliated with the University of London. The position was held by Professor Perceval Yetts until his retirement in 1946.

At the request of the palace officials in Beijing Sir Percival returned yet again to China in 1932 to organize another exhibition for them. But an event of far greater moment was the realization of Sir Percival's determination to bring to London some of the very pieces

3 Sir Percival consulting Chinese experts as they unpack items loaned to the International Exhibition at the Royal Academy in London in 1935.

he had helped to put on display in the Forbidden City, as well as those from the many other countries so eager to participate. This meant that Sir Percival would be organizing the greatest exhibition of Chinese art the world had ever seen. He enlisted the assistance of three renowned English experts on the subject, R.L. Hobson of the British Museum, George Eumorfopoulos and Oscar Raphael. They set out as a quartet on a global tour to complete arrangements for shipment to England of the most important Chinese treasures from all the countries on their itinerary (**2-5**).

Back in London, Sir Percival found the Royal Academy delighted to sponsor the exhibition, with the Earl of Lytton as Chairman of the Executive Committee. The Patrons were His Majesty the King, Her Majesty Queen Mary, and the President of the Republic of China. He was deeply gratified, too, when his dear friend and fellow collector, His Royal Highness The Crown Prince of Sweden, consented to be a member of the Committee of Honour. They had first met in China in 1924, and their mutual respect for the scholarship of the other was only to increase over the years as their connoisseurship in their respective chosen fields reached the level of intuitive perception.

4 Sir Percival and a visiting expert examining ancient bronzes sent from China to the International Exhibition in 1935.

The International Exhibition of Chinese Art opened at Burlington House in November 1935 (**6**). It was the first time that the full magnificence of the artistic tradition of China was revealed to the West. It is no exaggeration to say that without Sir Percival's skilful planning the exhibition might never have materialized. The only problem he and I had was in selecting from his own already splendid collection the objects which would go on display at Burlington House. Incidentally, Sir Percival's favourite piece in the final consignment of treasures he had acquired from the Yuin Yeh Bank in 1928 was chosen as the most beautiful ceramic object in this exhibition, and was illustrated in the colour frontispiece for the appropriate article in the *Burlington Magazine*. It is an exquisite pear-shaped Guan ware vase, the pale bluish-green glaze with wide irregular crackle stained golden brown (39).

The Collection had now grown to some 1,200 pieces, later to reach 1,400. Busy as we were in arranging and labelling them, I enrolled, at Sir Percival's suggestion, as a student of Chinese Art and Archaeology at the University of London with Professor Perceval Yetts. This widened my horizon considerably, giving me, in addition to my knowledge of ceramics, an interest in jade, sculpture, bronzes and epigraphy, an interest in which Sir Percival fully shared. One might truly say that a friendly 'rivalry' developed between my two professors, for each sought to outwit the other by reference to rare texts. I was the middleman, note-taking at the lectures from the one, and discussing the results with the

5 Dr F.T. Cheng (Special Commissioner of the Chinese Government), George Eumorfopoulos and Leigh
Ashton experimenting with an arrangement of some of the smaller ceramic items in the 1935-6 Exhibition – the majority of them loaned by Sir Percival David.

other. In summarizing the instruction I had received, and in preparation for the next
session, Sir Percival, with his superb library, was able to locate obscure references on the
subject, which sometimes confounded my teacher, although in certain cases the reverse
occurred.

The Burlington House Exhibition was the end of a chapter, and now it was time to
continue with our primary concern, namely, the assembling of a well documented
collection of Chinese ceramics which, with a reference library in Chinese and Western
languages, would be of great value to the serious student, while being of such aesthetic
quality as to be of interest to the general public.

So, until the outbreak of the Second World War, we were feverishly adding to the
material we had already amassed, with all the dated pieces we could find, while the
acquisition of objects in traditional Chinese taste continued – in subtle monochromes, in
designs boldly or finely delineated in underglaze blue and red, and in the delicately drawn
enamels featuring flowers and birds and with the occasional figure subject.

6 View of the 17th and 18th Century Gallery at the Royal Academy during the 1935-6 Exhibition. The large fish bowls on either side of the steps leading up to the throne were loaned to the Exhibition by Sir Percival David.

The War Years

The ambitious and exciting period of the 1930s was to terminate with the outbreak of the War in 1939, when the Collection and Library were crated and sent out of London to a place of comparative safety. Our contribution to the war effort was in an area completely unconnected with Chinese studies. Sir Percival, wishing to render his assistance to the most crucial front of the war, the aircraft industry, began studying the various types then in production. To further his investigations, we went in 1940 to the United States, where a valuable year was spent in visiting aircraft factories. After much deliberation, Sir Percival decided that the British 'Mosquito' was the machine he most favoured; it was to become one of the most versatile fighter-bombers of the war. He made a financial contribution to the construction of the Mosquito, and this compensated to a certain degree for his bitter disappointment in not being able to participate actively in the war because of ill health.

Our ultimate destination was India, and we travelled from Los Angeles to Hawaii in a top-class aircraft, accompanied by several high-ranking military personnel. Our departure from the island was not a simple matter. At 5.00 a.m. we boarded a sea-plane, the 'China Clipper', for Manila. The aircraft was in fact a model of the prototype we had seen at the Kaiser Aircraft Factory in Baltimore, Maryland, and we were told that as an active vehicle it was virtually out of service! It took three weeks to reach our destination after returning to base several times because of rough weather, which prevented the landing of a sea-plane. We continued the journey by plane from Manila to Hong Kong and thence by boat to Shanghai to liaise with other dedicated patriots.

In December 1941, at the time of Pearl Harbour, we unfortunately found ourselves still in Shanghai, and were interned by the Japanese. Under their supervision, however, we were permitted to visit old Chinese friends and collectors. These excursions were indeed welcome, and I took copious notes of all I saw and heard. We knew that, as diplomats, we would eventually be released, so in the meantime we discussed at great length the ultimate disposition of the David Collection. It would of course have been a most desirable addition to any museum, but donating it to such an institution would have meant combining it with existing collections and not keeping it as a separate entity in a building where its own artistic and academic identity would be preserved.

In August 1942, with other American and British personnel of similar status, we were exchanged for an equal number of Japanese citizens held at Lourenço Marques, Mozambique, the Portuguese colony on the east coast of Africa. From there we travelled to Johannesburg for medical treatment. Sir Percival had developed the crippling disease of amyotophic lateral sclerosis, which had begun manifesting itself during our nine months of internment. Although only in its early stages, there was nothing known at that time which would arrest its advance.

It was, however, our great fortune to find a number of Chinese art collectors in Johannesburg and, together with the enthusiastic support of the Chinese Ambassador and members of the provincial legislature, we organized an exhibition in aid of Chinese War Relief. It was an outstanding success, and financially most rewarding.

We then travelled to Cape Town, where we met Judge Davis of the Supreme Court, a fellow collector of Chinese ceramics with an excellent library of books on the subject, literally an oasis in a desert. He was delighted to meet Sir Percival, and we became close friends. We met as often as his Court commitments permitted, and it was wonderful for us to see and handle his treasures after what had seemed an eternity away from Chinese ceramics.

Our friendship with Judge Davis soon reached a degree of such intimacy that it might have been one of many years' duration rather than one of comparative brevity. At our meetings, topics of every description were discussed including, naturally, plans for the disposition of Sir Percival's Collection and Library. We were the beneficiaries of the Judge's wise counsel, which added a new perspective and a fresh impetus to our own belief that the Collection and Library should remain a separate entity. It was the Judge, in fact, who drew up the draft for the type of document which would ultimately be required for such a scheme, and which was indeed used almost word for word in the final Agreement.

Judge Davis travelled with us to the United States in 1945, where we visited museums in Washington, D.C., New York and Boston, and in Toronto, Canada. Here he saw sixteen of Sir Percival's finest pieces, these having originally been sent in 1938 for exhibition to the Fogg Art Museum, Harvard University, and subsequently on loan to Toronto. After the outbreak of the war, it was deemed that they would be safer there, and so they had remained in Toronto, giving pleasure to a new audience. Judge Davis then had to return to Cape Town, and we went back to the States to attend special clinics in different parts of the country. In every city we travelled through we never failed to visit all museums and collections of Chinese art. Even in America, the treatment for amyotophic lateral sclerosis was still at a rudimentary stage, and had no lasting effect. For the rest of his life Sir Percival was confined to a wheelchair, and fought a courageous battle against increasing disability. But he never deviated from his passion for Chinese art and literature; nor, for that matter, were his other pursuits abandoned. We managed despite his illness to travel to Europe, the United States, Hong Kong, Taiwan and Japan.

7 Sir Percival David with His Majesty King Gustaf VI Adolf of Sweden at the Drottningholm Palace Theatre in 1963.

The Post-War Years: Friendships and Travels

Sir Percival's old friend, His Royal Highness The Crown Prince of Sweden, became King Gustaf VI Adolf in 1950, and even before the Foundation opened he made several visits to London to examine the Collection as it emerged from crate to daylight. It was an ideal situation for handling and discussing pieces, and his connoisseurship helped us identify and date wares and to devise ways to elucidate the various types and periods of ceramics. On 19 May 1955 His Majesty received an Honorary D. Litt from Oxford University. The ceremony was held at the Sheldonian Theatre. Sir Percival and I were the guests of His Majesty and Queen Louise, and later attended a banquet hosted by the Chancellor. In the evening His Majesty graciously took the chair at a lecture I delivered on the Foundation. Afterwards His Majesty addressed the select audience, and paid tribute to the munificence of Sir Percival's benefaction to the University of London, and to his outstanding scholastic attainments. The lecture was repeated the following day to an audience of professors and senior students. On this occasion His Majesty was again present, although Sir Percival now took the chair, and delivered a most moving address on his long and deeply rewarding friendship with the Swedish monarch.

Over the next thirteen years we were frequently the guests of His Majesty and Queen Louise, sister of Earl Mountbatten. We were thus able to study the Royal Collection, and those belonging to his friends, as well as of the two national museums.

Our last visit to Sweden was in 1963 for the official opening by His Majesty of the Museum of Far Eastern Antiquities (**7** and **8**). In conjunction with this event a six-day seminar on Chinese art was held, and a special exhibition

8 Sir Percival and Lady David in Sweden in 1963.

of celadon and jade arranged. Sir Percival gave a fascinating account of his early collecting days in China and in London, and I completed the theme by describing the pieces which eventually made up the Foundation Collection as it now existed. A visit to Ekolsund, the 18th century palace residence of Dr and Mrs Carl Kempe, fifty-five kilometres from Stockholm, was arranged for us to see their superb collection of Chinese white wares of the 10th to the 18th century. On the last evening we saw a delightful rendition of the comic opera *Deceit Outwitted* by Haydn and Coltellini at the Drottningholm Palace Theatre, erected in 1766 as an annex to the Royal Summer Palace. Afterwards we attended a supper party hosted by Their Majesties at the China Slott (Chinese Pavilion), built in 1753. This truly rococo piece of chinoiserie was presented to Queen Louisa Ulrika by King Adolf Fredrik, who had it built in secret and bestowed, as if by magic, to the Queen on her birthday. It is filled with Chinese handicrafts acquired by succeeding Swedish monarchs since 1632, and has for many years been the Royal Family's favourite summer retreat. It provided a spectacular climax to our memorable visit.

I am extremely proud that His Majesty graciously continued our friendship after my husband's death in 1964. His Majesty came to London every year, and I made several visits to Stockholm as his guest until he, too, sadly passed away nine years later.

I had been actively engaged in keeping records of precisely dated Chinese antiquities since meeting Sir Percival in 1931. This work was continued during our internment in Shanghai and I was able to devote more time to it after I retired as Curator of the Foundation in 1959. It was not really until I became a widow, however, that the project could receive my full attention, and this happened to coincide with the time when His Majesty had also become interested in the subject. He enthusiastically encouraged me to escalate the work for early publication. My desire to include as many objects as were then known necessitated world-wide travel. This I accomplished with the continued inspiration of His Majesty, and I can truthfully say that the book would not have been completed without his support. It was therefore appropriate that the dedication should read 'In memory of His Majesty King Gustaf VI Adolf of Sweden, 1882-1973'.

In 1955 Sir Percival and I made one of our frequent visits to Paris. It was always a pleasure to see Michel Calmann, an old friend and a fellow inhabitant of our Oriental art world. On this occasion we paid a visit to his 'shooting box' – as the French call a hunting lodge – the centre of which he had converted into a gazebo-like setting for his beautiful Chinese porcelain.

Michel, no longer a young man, was concerned with the ultimate destination of his renowned collection. He greatly admired the munificence of Sir Percival's gift to the University of London and the fact that the objective had been achieved in his lifetime. As an active member of the Board of Governors of the Musée Guimet and their principal adviser on Chinese art, Michel considered this establishment the proper venue for his collection. His target had obviously been set by the perfection of Sir Percival's pieces, and he was duly modest about the quality of his own. He admitted to having, on occasion, been obliged to buy several objects in a group when he had only wanted one, so there were items that should be discarded, if he were to make the gift worthy of his reputation. For such a contingency, he recognized that only Sir Percival's discerning eye could weed out those that did not belong. The selection was made in an atmosphere of cheerful good humour, and for the objects to be donated, Michel designed an even more gem-like arrangement. Ill health delayed his worthy intentions, but he did live to see his collection installed as he wished, at the Guimet, the foremost museum of Oriental art in Paris.

We next went to Zürich, home to the famous Van de Heydt Collection of early Chinese bronzes. In Athens we visited the Benaki Museum, with its collection of Chinese art, and the donor's home with its diverse contents – both furnishings and decorative arts.

In 1956 we travelled to Taiwan. This was perhaps the most breathtaking of all our journeys, for here was the Imperial Collection which had been ferried from the mainland in 1948 by the United States Air Force. It was contained in ninety-five crates, and housed in mountain caves at Taizhong. We spent six months there, visiting the caves each day when the custodians opened a veritable Aladdin's hide-away for our delectation. Never again would we see so many objects of the highest quality day after day for such an extended period. On our second visit a Chinese-style museum had been built on the outskirts of Taibei, and a marvellous visual display greeted our arrival. The objects were the same, but the tantalizing atmosphere of the caves was somewhat diminished.

In 1957 we made a long visit to Japan to see an exhibition of Chinese ceramics, and the many outstanding collections formed by institutions and individuals. The subject has been pursued with the utmost vigour in Japan since the Tang dynasty, and its vogue extended to all parts of the country. There were indeed some outstanding museum and private collections, each item having been chosen with the customary regard to perfection that is so ingrained a characteristic of the Japanese people.

In 1958 we were invited by Avery Brundage, President of the Olympic Association and Committee (1952-72), to his home in Chicago for Sir Percival to appraise his collection of Chinese art. He had been a frequent visitor to the Foundation, and hoped to assemble pieces of like quality. Sir Percival naturally complied with his request, but unfortunately found that considerable weeding out was necessary. It was therefore a difficult assignment, but our host was infinitely grateful for the opinion, and proceeded to form an excellent assemblage of all phases of Chinese ceramics, and with a handsome financial donation added a wing to the H.M. De Young Memorial Museum in San Francisco, thus making it at that time the premier establishment for Chinese art on the West Coast of the United States.

While in Chicago we naturally visited the Art Institute, with, amongst its wealth of Chinese treasures, the justly famous Russell Tyson Collection. We were also recommended to explore the Field Museum of Natural History. It sounded a somewhat unlikely venue for Oriental objects, but it did give us a pleasant surprise with its interesting selection of ink cakes, inkstones, rhinoceros horn cups, and lacquer utensils.

In 1959 it was Florence, our favourite Italian city, for European painting came a close second to Chinese art in our esteem for the highest artistic achievement of the world. On an earlier visit to the city, we had been introduced to three collections of Chinese porcelain. On this occasion we investigated the possibility of some Chinese objects in the country finding a home in the Uffizi Gallery. The Director's determination was equal to Sir Percival's, and we were rewarded with the discovery of a group of 14th century celadon dishes and several rhinoceros horn cups in the storage area. What was unusual about the latter were the European silver gilt mounts embellishing these collector's items. They were the only known rhinoceros objects to be so enhanced, and started us on a search for others with similar ornamentation. To date, however, none has been discovered.

In 1960 we went again to the United States and made New York – always our best loved city – the focal point from which to visit several other centres of Chinese art. On arrival, the Metropolitan Museum of Art was our first destination, for it is very well endowed with treasures of every description in our particular areas of interest, especially in the field of Chinese ceramics which owes much to such pioneers as Altman, Bahr and Peters. Among the private collections, those of Myron and Pauline Falk and of Margot Holmes rank way above all others.

In Cleveland we were house guests of the Severance Millikins, owners of an exquisite collection of Chinese ceramics. In Kansas City we saw the famous Chinese collection of the William Nelson Rockhill Gallery of Art. On our return to the East Coast we were house guests of the Paul Bernats in Boston; their collection of Qing dynasty enamelled wares was unequalled in quality save by those in the Foundation. The collections of the Museum of Fine Arts, Boston, and the Fogg Art Museum range from Shang bronzes to 18th century porcelain, each important in its own way. The second last stop on our itinerary was Washington, D.C. To see and study the celebrated Chinese collection of the Freer Gallery of Art was a splendid conclusion to what was to be Sir Percival's last trip to the States.

We returned to London via New York where we attended a party for Chinese art collectors at Margot Holmes' apartment. We met again with our old friend Hershel Johnson, the first United States representative at the United Nations and an already established connoisseur of 18th century porcelain. He was to form a representative collection of this period. When he was United States Ambassador to Brazil, we visited him in Rio de Janeiro and were delighted at the quality of the porcelain he had been able to acquire and the enthusiasm with which he pursued the subject.

In 1960 we attended the 25th Congress of Orientalists in Moscow. It was an exhilarating experience to meet so many Orientalists from all over the world with a common tongue – English. We also visited Leningrad, and the fabulous Hermitage Museum with its fifteen miles of rooms and passages, crammed with superb works of art of every age and of every country.

The Donation to the University of London

Sir Percival's intense interest in and profound knowledge of Chinese ceramics enabled him to form an unrivalled collection from the ceramic kilns of China, and he wanted, above all else, to find a suitable home for it, so that it would be an instrument of teaching for serious-minded students and, at the same time, be available for public viewing.

In 1950, while still in the United States, Sir Percival corresponded with the Vice Chancellor of the University of London, Dame Lillian Penson, offering as a gift to the University this veritable treasure of a collection, together with his incomparable library of Chinese and Western books, provided that certain conditions be met. The University was delighted and agreed that both should be housed together in a separate Foundation bearing Sir Percival's name, and that it should be administered by its own staff under the School of Oriental and African Studies.

The Percival David Foundation of Chinese Art was opened to the public on 10 June 1952. The Chair of Chinese Art and Archaeology which Sir Percival had established at the Courtauld Institute and which was held by Professor Perceval Yetts until his retirement in

1946 was now transferred to the School of Oriental and African Studies, and the holder of the Chair was to be concurrently the Head of the Foundation. I became the Foundation's first Curator and retained the post until 1959.

In forming his unique collection Sir Percival chose to set certain limits upon his own selection, deliberately leaving blanks where he knew that these were being filled by other collectors. Shortly before the Foundation opened, it was offered and accepted one such group consisting of 150 monochrome porcelains which had been collected by the Honourable Mountstuart Elphinstone. The group complements Sir Percival's own and considerably enchances the importance of the Collection's monochromes.

Foreign Loans

The first loan from the Foundation to a foreign city was that to the Venice exhibition of Chinese art, 'Mostra D'Arte Cinese', held in 1954 to celebrate the septicentennial of the birth of Marco Polo. Thirteen pieces were selected from the Foundation, along with eight pieces from our own newly acquired treasures. The exhibition was wide in scope, ranging from Shang bronzes to Qing monochromes and enamelled porcelain, but the emphasis was on items produced in the last quarter of the 13th century, when Marco Polo was engaged in the diplomatic service of Kublai Khan.

The largest loan of objects from the Foundation to a foreign country took place in 1980, when one hundred of our most beautiful specimens travelled to Japan. The exhibition opened at the National Museum in Tokyo on 3 June, and attracted more visitors than even a display of selected items from the fabulous Shōsō-in Repository in Nara. Our exhibition then travelled to the National Museum in Kyoto, and to the City Museum in Nagoya, and in both places the reception was equally enthusiastic. The Japanese had for centuries been ardent and informed collectors of Chinese art, and were particularly able to appreciate the magnificent treasures from the Foundation.

A recent loan from the Foundation to the United States was in 1987, when we exhibited seven of our best celadon pieces in the Indianapolis Museum of Art. They attracted much attention, and the impact has been a remarkably enthusiastic response from other art institutions. As this guide goes to press, we are arranging to send a selection of fifty-eight pieces to four American museums: the Los Angeles County Museum, the Kimball Art Museum in Fort Worth, Texas, the Virginia Museum of Fine Arts in Richmond, and the Museum of Fine Arts, Boston. The exhibitions will last from the summer of 1989 to the summer of 1990, and will undoubtedly bring American audiences an even greater degree of awareness of both the superb quality of the Foundation's Chinese ceramics and its unique character.

Recent Developments

On 19 April 1983 Her Royal Highness The Princess Royal honoured the Foundation by

9 Lady David in the Lady David Gallery which was opened in 1983.

officiating at the ceremony to open the Lady David Gallery and the Library extension. These additions were the most significant development in the history of the Foundation since its opening in 1952, and were made possible by financing from the University Court and the donor's widow, and by a contribution from the Nihon Keizai Shimbun in recognition of the very successful exhibition of one hundred items from the Foundation's collection in Japan in 1980. The new Gallery adds nearly half as much again to the exhibition space, and introduces a new element by permitting the rotation of objects on display from their normal arrangement to form individual groups for specialized study (**9**). The Library too, has benefited equally from the increased area, and for the first time is safely and accessibly housed.

Another milestone in the history of the Foundation was reached in 1988, when on 23 May the Lady David Seminar Centre was officially opened by The Lord Flowers, the Vice Chancellor of the University of London. This event may be considered as the concluding episode in the sequence of developments that led to the formation of this unique institution as a display and research centre for the study of Chinese art and archaeology. With the Lady David Seminar Centre, Sir Percival's ambition, which was first conceived in China sixty years ago, is finally being fulfilled because, in addition to the other facilities there is an area for teaching, research, and visiting lecturers, and a venue for the gathering of affiliated societies.

Sir Percival's Research

As a scholar Sir Percival made significant contributions to the study of Chinese ceramics and Chinese connoisseurship, as well as other fields of Chinese study. He became immersed in the literary accomplishments of the Chinese with the same enthusiasm that he had for their artistic attainments. It was his discovery of the *Ge Gu Yao Lun* (A Discussion of the Essential Criteria of Antiquities), an encyclopaedia of art and archaeology compiled in the

14th century, that motivated his desire to interpret Chinese connoisseurship for a Western audience. His research focused on the translation of the work into English, an undertaking which would illuminate the Westerner's understanding of the Chinese scholar-collector's appreciation of true perfection in art.

It was in the course of his research on Ru ware (the result of which was published in 'A Commentary on Ju Ware' in the *Transactions of the Oriental Ceramic Society* in 1937) that Sir Percival discovered this 14th century compendium. The author's deliberations accorded so precisely with his own thinking that Sir Percival decided that his fellow students could benefit from a complete rendition of the text. Delving into the bibliographical background of this intriguing work proved tantalizing. Consultation with two eminent Sinologists, Professor Paul Pelliot of Paris, and Dr Arthur Hummel of the Library of Congress, Washington, D.C., elicited only the information that the first edition of Cao Zhao's text in three chapters, of the Hongwu period, was referred to in an enlarged edition of the work, in thirteen chapters, believed to have been first published in 1459. Both scholars, however, had been unable to trace a copy of the first edition and expressed doubts that it still existed. Imagine our good fortune, then, to discover and acquire such a rarity while interned in Shanghai in 1942.

Sir Percival's long wait was rewarded by his acquisition of the first edition of 1388, consisting of three chapters in Cao Zhao's original order. It had come from the Pan family in Suzhou and was impressed with their seals and those of the Qing bibliophile Mo Youzhi (1811-71). Sir Percival translated both the 1388 and the 1459 editions, and to clarify the subject, entitled his work *Chinese Connoisseurship*.

Another major area of research was the 13th century traveller, Marco Polo. Sir Percival's fascination with the life of Marco Polo was given a focus by the search for an unknown manuscript by the Venetian recounting his travels to China. This he finally traced to the library in the Monastery of San Lorenzo de la Escorial, some fifty kilometres from Madrid, built like a gigantic parallelogram beneath four peaked towers. Encouraged in his search by the enthusiastic assistance of the Chaplain of the Biblioteca National, Madrid, and the Senior Notary of Toledo, Don Agustin Garcia Guisasola, he located the requisite item in their extensive inventories, only to discover that the numerically catalogued volume had been misplaced. Tracing the elusive manuscript occupied many weeks, but success was finally achieved when he was at last able to gaze in awe at the precious tome.

Sir Percival then set about publishing his important document and financed a definitive edition of *The Travels of Marco Polo* in two volumes, prepared in collaboration with two professors, Paul Pelliot of Paris and Christopher Moule of Cambridge. The text of this first edition is reproduced in Volume I, and is enhanced by a facsimile of the hand-coloured frontispiece which embellishes the original manuscript.

Yet another facet of Chinese life that engaged Sir Percival's interest was the rather unusual courier service operating in that country and its overseas connections. This interest naturally involved a detailed knowledge of China's geography and history, and widened his perspective of China in general and, in particular his appreciation of the complex communication problems between the peoples of this vast country. Mail travelling to inland recipients merely necessitated the fixing of a local adhesive, whereas a letter destined for abroad required full payment at the place of origin to cover its entire journey. The local adhesive conveyed it to a maritime city, such as Beijing or Shanghai, where the requisite foreign stamp would be applied, and the town of origin reimbursed for the amount in excess of the inland charge. We thus have a record of the various routes used for the quickest delivery of letters, which often reveals just what conditions were prevailing during transit.

Sir Percival's interest dramatically changed the approach to Chinese philately, and international exhibitions began to flourish, so keenly was the subject adopted as a full-time pursuit. We were the recipients of several Gold Medals for our work on the subject of Chinese philately, and again Sir Percival became the doyen of acknowledged experts on this fascinating topic.

In addition to these and other Chinese subjects, Sir Percival studied in depth two groups of objects of European provenance. One was early 18th century English silver and furniture, and the other the work of the French mechanician and watchmaker, Abraham-Louis Brequet (1747-1823). In 1775 Brequet established a shop in Paris, where he built instruments of great accuracy, including astronomical clocks and marine chronometers; he also initiated improvements in watches by the use of the ruby as bearing. Sir Percival was the proud owner of two of these, one being the first example of a *perpetuelle* or self-winding watch.

Sir Percival David was indeed a gifted individual, blessed with taste and intellect, and the energy to garner these to good purpose. The Foundation of Chinese Art that bears his name is a monument to his vision and generosity, a gem in a city of great museums and institutions of learning.

In concluding his address at the opening ceremony of the Percival David Foundation of Chinese Art, Sir Ralph Turner, the Director of the School of Oriental and African Studies, said:

> A princely gift has been made to the University, a Collection of unique value and beauty.
> In a future age, when we have all passed from this scene, some visitor to the Foundation may ask, 'Who and what sort was the man whose name this Foundation bears?'
> Surrounded by these superb examples of the art of a distant people and a distant age, to the collection and study of which that man devoted his life, our visitor will be well answered by the epitaph of Sir Christopher Wren in St. Paul's, London: '*Si monumentum requiris circumspice* [If you seek his monument look around].'

Kiln Sites

Chronology

Chinese Dynasties and Periods

Neolithic period	c. 7000 - 1600 BC
Shang dynasty	c. 1600 - 1027 BC
Western Zhou	1027 - 771 BC
Eastern Zhou	770 - 256 BC
Spring and Autumn period	770 - 476 BC
Warring States period	475 - 221 BC
Qin dynasty	221 - 206 BC
Western Han	206 BC - AD 8
Xin dynasty (Wang Mang interregnum)	9 - 23
Eastern Han	25 - 220
Six Dynasties period	220 - 580
Northern and Southern dynasties	420 - 580
Sui dynasty	581 - 618
Tang dynasty	618 - 907
Liao dynasty	907 - 1125
Five dynasties period	907 - 960
Song dynasty	960 - 1279
Northern Song	960 - 1127
Southern Song	1127 - 1279
Jin dynasty	1115 - 1234
Yuan dynasty	1279 - 1368
Ming dynasty	1368 - 1644
Qing dynasty	1644 - 1911
Republic	1912 - 1949
People's Republic	1949 -

Reign Periods of the Ming and Qing Dynasties

Ming

Hongwu	1368-1398	Hongzhi	1488-1505
Jianwen	1399-1402	Zhengde	1506-1521
Yongle	1403-1424	Jiajing	1522-1566
Hongxi	1425	Longqing	1567-1572
Xuande	1426-1435	Wanli	1573-1620
Zhengtong	1436-1449	Taichang	1620
Jingtai	1450-1457	Tianqi	1621-1627
Tianshun	1457-1464	Chongzhen	1628-1644
Chenghua	1465-1487		

Qing

Shunzhi	1644-1661	Daoguang	1821-1850
Kangxi	1662-1722	Xianfeng	1851-1861
Yongzheng	1723-1735	Tongzhi	1862-1874
Qianlong	1736-1795	Guangxu	1875-1908
Jiaqing	1796-1820	Xuantong	1909-1911

The Foundation and the Galleries

The aim of this guide to the Collection is to provide the visitor with an introduction to the unique collection of Chinese ceramics in the Percival David Foundation. Lady David in her Introduction has painted a portrait of the remarkable man who built the Collection and has told the story of the Percival David Foundation's development. In the following chapters it is intended to give an indication of the scope of the Collection, place the pieces in their broad historical context and highlight a few of the most important items.

First, however, it may be useful to give the reader a general view of the physical layout of the Foundation, and in doing this we will start at basement level and travel upwards. Lady David has mentioned that Sir Percival David gave to the University of London not only his world famous collection of Chinese ceramics, but also his remarkable library of books pertaining to Chinese art. In addition to books in European languages this library also includes books in Chinese and Japanese. The Chinese volumes are very varied and in a number of cases extremely rare. They include local gazetteers (local histories) of most of the main ceramic-producing areas of China, while on the other hand there are

10
A page from the *Cheng Shi Moyuan* published in 1606.

collections of essays on numerous aspects of Chinese art, as well as some especially rare volumes containing early examples of Chinese colour printing. A particularly fine book in the latter category is the *Cheng Shi Moyuan* (Mr Cheng's Ink Garden), printed in 1606. This is a collection of designs for ink cakes, a number of which are shown in colour (**10**). The illustrations were produced by woodblock printing methods; the different colours were all applied using the same printing block, with each colour carefully applied to its own section of the block. Among the European books are scholarly works on Chinese art, privately printed catalogues of individual collections (many now dispersed), and some fascinating books on China published by missionary societies which sent representatives to China in the 17th and 18th centuries. This library, which is housed in the basement of the Foundation, is an

11
The Lady David Gallery
during the exhibition held
to commemorate the 50th
anniversary of the 1935-6
Exhibition. All the pieces
loaned by Sir Percival to
the Exhibition in 1935 and
which are now in the Per-
cival David Foundation
were displayed together.

invaluable source of reference for students of Chinese art. It is not
generally open to the public, but anyone wishing to consult the books
therein may apply to the Curator for a special reader's ticket.

For most visitors to the Foundation, however, the first area of
interest is the ground floor. The Lady David Gallery was opened in 1983,
thanks to the generosity of Lady David and a contribution by the Nihon
Keizai Shimbun, and this gallery provides attractive modern display
space which is utilized in a number of ways. It is sometimes used as a
primary gallery where examples of the various types of ceramic ware in
the Collection can be displayed to provide an overall introduction to the
ceramics in the Foundation. At other times it is used for special exhibitions, such as that mounted in 1985 to celebrate the 50th anniversary of
that seminal event, the International Exhibition of Chinese Art held in
London in 1935-6, of which Sir Percival was Director and to which he was
the major private contributor (**11**). This is also the only gallery where
it is possible to display in appropriately controlled conditions a fascinating recent acquisition, a painting very generously presented to the Foundation in 1986 by Lady David (**12**). The label gives the title of the
painting as *Guwan tu* (Scroll of Antiquities), and states that the scroll is

sixth in a series. Dated by inscription to the year 1728, this very long handscroll is the work of an anonymous court artist and depicts objects of art from the Imperial Collection in the reign of the emperor Yong-zheng. These pieces of jade, metalwork and ceramics are painted in painstaking detail and shown displayed on their traditional carved wooden stands. A wide range of ceramic items from the Imperial Collection is shown on the scroll; a number of these relate very closely to items in the Foundation's collection, some of which may indeed be the actual pieces depicted on the painting. Whenever the scroll is on display, therefore, some of the related items are displayed in the connecting pier cases.

On the first floor is the gallery that houses the early monochrome wares together with some later wares made in imitation of them, and also a small number of early black wares and pieces of the Cizhou and Yixing types. The majority of the pieces on this floor date to the Song and Yuan periods, but there are some Yue wares of the Six Dynasties period, some Longquan celadon wares of the Ming dynasty, and some Qing

12
Detail of the *Scroll of Antiquities* (dated 1728) showing objects of jade, bronze and stoneware and two wood *ruyi* sceptres with jade inlays and yellow silk tassels. Colours on paper. Height 62.5 cm. Gift of Lady David.

dynasty celadons made at Jingdezhen in imitation of the earlier wares. The northeast wall is devoted to Ding and other early white wares, with some later imitations. The cases beside the door contain black wares from several provinces, and other white wares. The east end of the gallery has a display of Jun wares, a number of which, with their dramatic purple splashes, cannot strictly be called monochromes but indicate the direction of the development of this interesting ware. The east section of the south wall has a case containing the remarkable collection of Ru wares and some of the Guan ware pieces. These latter are continued in the cases on the west side of the south wall, along with copies of Guan ware made in the Ming and Qing dynasties. The remainder of the west end of this gallery is devoted to Longquan celadons, with the exception of two cases which contain Yue and Yaozhou wares, and some examples of Qing dynasty celadon-glazed porcelains. The examples of Yixing and Cizhou wares are in small side cases on the south side of the gallery. All the ceramic types mentioned in this brief description of the layout of the collection will be discussed in the following chapters, as parts of a chronological account of the development of Chinese ceramics.

Most of the wares displayed on the first floor have rather muted colours and subtle decoration, often relying for their impact on simplicity and elegance of form and glaze. In contrast the wares on the second floor present to the eye a riot of colours and designs. Here are displayed the wares decorated in underglaze blue alongside their underglaze red counterparts. These are in the east section of the gallery, as are those *doucai* and *wucai* pieces that combine underglaze blue and overglaze enamel designs. In this section too is a variety of Ming dynasty enamelled wares in a number of different styles. In the central area of the gallery are the cases containing many of the 18th century monochrome wares presented to the Foundation in 1952 by the Honourable Mountstuart Elphinstone, which complement so well Sir Percival's own collection. In the west area of the gallery are the later white wares from both the Jingdezhen and Dehua kilns, as well as the magnificent collection of copper red wares. The famous collection of Ming and Qing monochrome yellow wares face green and overglaze iron red examples on the opposite side of the gallery. Lastly, in the southwest part of this gallery are to be found the exquisite overglaze enamel decorated wares of the late 17th and 18th centuries, including those known as *famille verte* and *famille rose*.

The Early Wares

3rd - 10th century

Although the majority of the pieces in the Foundation date to the period spanning the late 10th century to the 18th century (Song to Qing dynasty), Sir Percival did acquire some important examples of earlier wares. These early pieces are interesting not only in themselves but also as indicators of the development of Chinese high-fired, glazed ceramics before the Song period. The group of Yue wares is a case in point. These include some of the earliest items in the Collection, from the late 3rd century, as well as some of the refined wares of the 10th century. Yue wares have a greenish alkaline glaze, which could be fired to the same high temperature as the stoneware body material. The body is fine, compact and greyish in colour. This grey body colour was important because the glaze was thin and fairly transparent, so that the body colour seen through the glaze affected its colour, giving it a softer tone. All the wares in the Yue group come from a region in east China centring on Zhejiang province. It was a region inhabited by a minority people known as the

13
Early Yue ware basin.
3rd or early 4th century.
Diameter 33.1 cm.
PDF 250

Yue, although the region itself changed its name frequently over the period concerned. Strictly speaking only the pieces made during the time when the region was controlled by the small state of Wu-Yue should be called Yue ware. This was in the 10th century when these wares were also sent as tribute to the Chinese court at Kaifeng. However the appellation early Yue has also been adopted for the material produced in the preceding centuries.

The pieces of the 3rd and 4th centuries, while lacking the refinement of their successors, nevertheless display considerable mastery of

33

materials and provide interesting insight into the development of decorative techniques. The large basin (**13**), which dates to the Western Jin period, was probably the product of the kilns in the Shaoxing area. The design inside the basin is of two fish simply incised in outline with pecking marks indicating the scales. The fish is traditionally a symbol of plenty in China. As well as the incising on the inside of this basin, two more decorative techniques are employed on the outside. A diamond diaper band has been impressed into the surface of the clay with a rouletting tool, and this band is punctuated by four low-relief masks, which have been sprig-moulded and then applied to the surface of the vessel. The relief masks are made in the form of the monster mask (*taotie*) ring handles found on bronze vessels. In the case of the ceramic version the ring handles are not handles in any practical sense and are purely decorative.

Similar use of decorative techniques can be seen on the jar (**14**) which was probably manufactured at the Jiuyan kilns. The same type of rouletted design can be seen on the shoulders of this jar, but here the rouletted band is enclosed between two bands of impressed circles – almost certainly produced with the end of a bamboo tube. This vessel also has sprig-moulded elements punctuating the bands, but in this instance a small Buddha figure is depicted. Vessels of this type, together with bronze mirrors of the period, carry some of the earliest depictions of the Buddha in the Chinese decorative arts. Among these early green wares zoomorphic themes were also popular, as can be seen from the lampstand (**15**).

14
Early Yue ware jar. Late 3rd or early 4th century. Height 12.5 cm. PDF A200

15
Early Yue ware lamp-stand. 4th century. Height 11 cm. PDF A202

In this instance the precision of the wheel-thrown base section (with impressed rouletted decoration on its horizontal rim) and the upper shallow bowl can be contrasted with the rather freely modelled seated bear that acts as the central column. The bear with one paw to its face is in a somewhat naturalistic pose, and an attempt at depiction of fur has been made by the ceramic decorator using the old-established techniques of pecking and striating.

16
Yue ware bowl with carved and incised decoration, the mouthrim bound with base gold. 10th century. Diameter 14.5 cm.
PDF 246

The Foundation is fortunate in having a number of examples of early Zhejiang green wares, and it also has some fine examples of the later type that may more properly be given the name Yue wares. While these late 9th or 10th century examples have a thin greenish glaze in common with the early Yue pieces discussed above, the glaze of later examples is much more even and somewhat more silvery in tone. The latter is the result of a more precise control of both the glaze components and the reducing atmosphere in the kiln during firing. Among these Yue wares are some which retain the remains of gold or silver bands. These were of the type known as *bise yao* (reserved colour wares) which were sent by the ruling house of Wu-Yue as gifts to neighbouring states, and as tribute to the imperial Song court at Kaifeng between 974 and 990. One such piece is the bowl (**16**) , on which can still be seen a fragmentary band of base gold. On the outside of the bowl is a carved and incised design of stylized waves, while on the inside the wave motif is repeated, with a sea dragon's head emerging from the water in the

17
Yue bowl with carved
and incised decoration.
Late 9th or early 10th cen-
tury. Diameter 17.5 cm.
PDF 262

centre. The bowl was probably made at Shanglin Hu.

A flat-bottomed bowl of slightly earlier date, late 9th or early 10th century, has a number of interesting features (**17**). On the base of the bowl, the character *yong* (eternal) has been incised inside the five marks made by the stand on which it was fired, while the encircling footring is gracefully splayed in a manner we will also see on the Ru wares. On this second Yue bowl, which is probably a product of the kilns in Yuyao Xian, carved decoration has once again been used, but here the style is very bold and formal, producing a series of overlapping lotus petals frequently seen in metalwork of the Tang dynasty. This arrangement of petals on the outside of bowls became a recurring feature in the decoration of Chinese ceramics. How far the skill in incising decorative motifs had progressed since the time of the early Yue basin (13) can be seen on the inside of this bowl. A narrow band of scrolling decoration runs just below the rim, while in the centre is a very precisely executed design of two phoenixes circling a pearl. The very fine even lines of the incised design produce a rather subtle decorative effect, while the motif itself is strongly reminiscent of decoration on gold and silver wares of the Tang dynasty. This same style of decoration can be seen on a round box in the Collection (**18**). Its shape is characteristic of a type of box that was very popular in the late Tang period, and which is also found in precious metals. A plant-inspired scroll runs around the sides of the box while on the slightly domed lid the fine incised lines produce a ribbon decoration encircling a roundel containing a 'cash' motif and the four characters *fu shou chang yan*, which may be translated as 'happiness and longevity for ever'. The use

of characters, and particularly four characters to form an auspicious phrase, has remained a popular device in the decoration of ceramics in China.

The other important group of early wares in the Foundation is that of the white wares made in the north of China prior to and at the very beginning of the Song dynasty.

18
Yue ware box with incised decoration. Late 9th or early 10th century. Diameter 12.3 cm. PDF 267

19
White porcellanous bowl of 'Samarra' type. 9th century. Diameter 14.4 cm. PDF A107

These should be discussed briefly before a more comprehensive introduction to the Foundation's unrivalled collection of Ding wares is undertaken in the next chapter. Excavations carried out in China have now confirmed that a good quality, high-fired white ware was being produced in north China certainly in the 9th century and probably earlier. A number of questions still remain to be answered, and indeed in some cases recent investigations have raised as many new questions as they have answered old ones. A type of early white ware that has been the subject of scholarly debate is exemplified by the bowl (**19**). This kind of bowl is usually referred to as the 'Samarra' type since examples have been excavated from the early Islamic site at Samarra on the Euphrates in modern Iraq. This type of bowl is characterized by a rolled rim and a low, broad footring with a recessed centre. It has been covered with a white slip (watery clay mixture) and a colourless glaze. These 9th century bowls had previously been

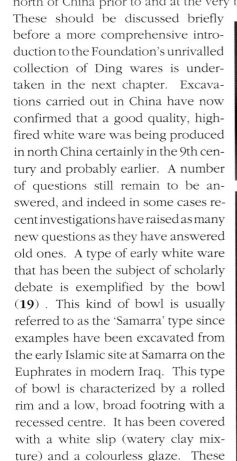

assumed to come from the Xing kilns in Henan province, but excavations at the Ding kilns at Quyang , Hebei province, have also unearthed bowls of this type, and the kilns at Gongxian in Henan province have yielded similar bowls.

Another early white ware bowl in the Collection (**20**) has been given a coating of slip only on the inside, and indeed the glaze on the outside does not reach the foot – a characteristic common on wares of the Tang period. The bowl is undecorated but the lip has been gently lobed by indenting the circular rim while the clay was still soft. This simple but effective device can also be seen on a 10th century Yue ware bowl in the Collection (PDF 214), although the latter piece has a much higher footring and is fully glazed. The transmission of ceramic technology between kilns and the influence of one kiln's decorative style and techniques on those of another are important aspects in the development of Chinese ceramics.

20
White porcellanous bowl with lobed rim. 9th or early 10th century. Diameter 17.9 cm. PDF A106

The Wares of North China in the Northern Song and the Jin Dynasty

960-1127 and 1115-1234

While it may be unwise to say that this or that was 'the favourite piece' of a certain collector, one feels justified in saying of Sir Percival David that he was particularly drawn to the classic wares of the Song dynasty. These subtle and refined wares (dating as they do from a period when European ceramic art was in its infancy) were the objects that stunned the visitors to the 1935-6 Exhibition – just as Sir Percival, the Exhibition's Director, intended they should. The fine pieces dating to this classic period that he lent to that exhibition constitute but a small part of this category of wares that he eventually gave to the University of London, and which form such an important part of the Collection as a whole.

It seems appropriate to begin the discussion of the wares produced in the north of China during this period with the white wares manufactured at the Ding kilns in Hebei province. The major product of these kilns in the Northern Song and the Jin dynasty was a high-fired white-bodied ware with a rich ivory glaze. Like the 10th century Yue ware, this was a ware that found favour with the court and there are records of Ding ware vessels being sent as tribute to the Song emperor as early as 980.

A change in the colour of the glaze on these early white wares can be seen at the end of the Five Dynasties period and the beginning of the Song dynasty. This was a change from a pure white or slightly bluish glaze tone to a warm ivory tone, and was due to a change from firing the wares in a reducing atmosphere (restricting the amount of oxygen in the kiln) to an oxidizing atmosphere (allowing an abundance of oxygen into the kiln). This period also saw the changeover from firing with wood to firing with coal.

One of the most immediately apparent features of Ding vessels is that the majority of open wares have their rims bound with a copper alloy (**21**) , or occasionally with a silver or gold band. As well as providing an aesthetically pleasing colour contrast to the ivory glaze, there were good practical reasons for the application of these metal rims. The ceramics were fired in saggars (clay boxes) that protected them from kiln debris (ash etc.) and ensured an even atmosphere around them. To give

21
Ding ware dish with combed and incised decoration, the mouth-rim bound with copper alloy. 11th-12th century. Diameter 22 cm. PDF 160

39

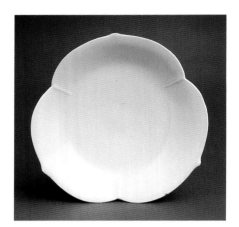

22
Ding ware trilobate dish.
10th century. Width
13.4 cm. PDF 173

each piece a separate saggar would have been most uneconomical in regard to space within the relatively small firing chamber of these kilns, which were of horseshoe shape and of the down-draught type. It was thus desirable to put several pieces in a single saggar. If the pieces were to stand on their footrims then they would, perforce, have to stand one on top of the other, marking the inside of the lower bowls. The solution was to have stepped saggars or saggars made of rings, with bowls or dishes standing on ridges on their mouthrims one above the other but not touching. This method, however, required that the mouthrim be wiped clean of glaze so that the molten glaze would not adhere to the inside of the saggar. When the vessels came out of the kiln, therefore, they had unglazed rims, which were then bound, usually with copper alloy that was cut from a sheet and then shaped around the rim so that there would be no unsightly join in the metal. This is the case for both plain and foliated rims.

The majority of the Ding wares in the Foundation have carved and incised decoration, as on the dish with bound rim (**21**). This dish has a fluently executed design of two ducks on a pond among reeds, the water being indicated by parallel wavy lines produced by a comb-like instrument. This dish is particularly interesting, since an examination of its profile reveals that it was thrown on the

23
Ding ware vase in 'teardrop' shape with carved and incised decoration.
11th-12th century. Height
36.5 cm. PDF 101

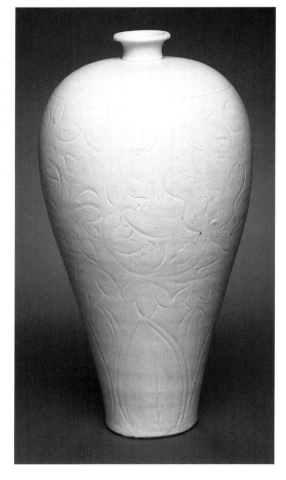

wheel, then the carved and incised decoration was applied, and finally the piece was put over a plain mould to give it its flared sides and the sharp angle between sides and base. What is remarkable is that this shaping was achieved without unduly compressing the decoration.

Many of the early Ding wares, produced before the adoption of the mouthrim firing technique, are undecorated and owe their appeal to the beauty of their glaze and shape. The small trilobate dish (**22**) is a particularly fine example dating to the 10th or early 11th century. The effect of its form – made up of three petals – has been enhanced by the application of fine slip lines under the glaze to continue the lobed effect from the rim into the sides. The dish has been fired on its footrim and has two characters *hui ji* incised through the glaze on its base, which may provide a clue to the patron who ordered this piece.

The largest proportion of Ding pieces are open wares (bowls, dishes and plates), but the Foundation is very fortunate in having a superb and rare example of a vase in 'tear-drop' shape with narrow neck, wide rounded shoulders and narrow foot (**23**). Like the dish (21), this vase also has carved and incised decoration. The popular Ding ware motif of overlapping petals appears on the shoulder, while a bold, freely drawn peony scroll decorates the central area with overlapping leaves around the foot. This division of the vessel into specific decorative zones is characteristic of Chinese ceramic decoration and becomes even more apparent on later wares.

During the late 11th or early 12th century moulds for imparting decorative designs to the inside of bowls and dishes were introduced at the Ding kilns. The designs were cut into the clay moulds *intaglio* so that when the soft clay of the vessel was pressed into the mould a decorative scheme in sharp low relief was produced on the inside of the bowl. (The use of moulds in this way also facilitated the production of bowls and dishes of uniform size for placing upside down in stepped or ring saggars.) The style of decoration found in moulded Ding wares differs dramatically from that seen on the carved and incised items. As can be seen from the bowl (**24**), the moulded wares have a much more crowded and formal style. On this bowl can also be noted the use of a minor decorative band, of a kind that is not usually employed on carved and incised examples. The band is also interesting in that it at first sight resembles one that in Europe would

24
Ding ware bowl with moulded decoration, the mouthrim bound with copper alloy. 12th century. Diameter 18 cm. PDF 108

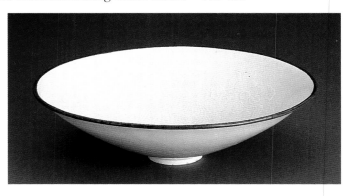

be called a Greek key or key-fret design. On closer inspection, however, it can be seen that the 12th century Chinese band is in fact composed of a series of individual squared spirals. The elegant and ornate phoenixes seen in this case against a background of peony scrolls are a popular motif used to great effect on moulded Ding wares. Indeed this same theme of phoenixes amongst flowers can be seen on a Ding mould in the Foundation's collection, which bears an inscription giving a date equivalent to 1184.

The moulded Ding bowl itself also bears a dated inscription but of a rather different type. This is one of a number of pieces in the Collection that have an imperial inscription that was added (often hundreds of years after the date of manufacture) when the piece was in the collection of the imperial family. One emperor in particular, the emperor Qianlong (1736-95), had a penchant for recording his appreciation of works of art by inscribing them and adding his seal. The poem on the base of this piece is one that also appears in *The Collected Works of the Emperor Qianlong,* Volume 86, Section IV. It is entitled 'On a bowl of Ding ware', and may be translated as follows:

> Amid accumulated pollen and massed flowers the two phoenixes droop their wings.
> The colour is confined to that prized by the Yin dynasty [i.e. white, which was the Yin imperial colour], simple and unadorned.
> It is not until we come down to the Zhu [Ming] dynasty of Xuan [Xuande] and Cheng [Chenghua] that we get elaborate painting and the employment of fine colours.
> Composed by Qianlong in the spring of the cyclical year *ding yu* [1777], and inscribed by imperial order.

The poem is followed by the mark of his seal reading *Tai bo* (great unpolished gem).

Although the Ding kilns are usually associated with white wares, some pieces with coloured glazes were also made there: green-glazed and brown-glazed wares, as well as a very rare and beautiful ware known as black Ding. The Foundation is fortunate in having an example of this latter type in perfect condition (**25**). While the body material is similar to the white pieces, and its thinly potted conical shape and small footring are also characteristic of the pale wares, this bowl has a thick, lustrous black glaze. The glaze has pooled in the bottom of the inside of the bowl, as it was fired on its footring, despite

25
Black Ding ware bowl with metal bound mouth-rim. 11th-12th century. Diameter 18.5 cm.
PDF 300

the fact that the mouthrim bears a metal band just like that seen on the pieces mentioned above which were fired upside down. The glaze on the outside does not reach as far as the foot of the vessel, and two finger marks can be seen on the edge of the glaze where it has been held for dipping into the vat of glaze. There is no decoration on the bowl as this would have been obscured by the dense black glaze.

26
Yaozhou ware box with carved and combed decoration. 11th century. Diameter 17.1 cm.
PDF 244

When the Ding wares eventually lost favour with the Northern Song court, their place was taken by another ware produced in north China during the Song dynasty, and also during the succeeding periods when northern China was under the control of foreign invaders – first the Jurchen Tartars and then the Mongols. This was the Northern Celadon ware produced at kilns in the Yaozhou area of Shaanxi province and also at kilns in Henan province, most notably those at Linru. Excavations carried out at these sites since the late 1950s have given us a much clearer picture of these wares, and the trend has therefore been to move away from calling them Northern Celadon wares, and towards designations indicating the kiln areas where they were likely to have been made. As far as can be ascertained in the light of present knowledge, the greatest variety and highest quality of these wares came from the Yaozhou kilns, but pieces very similar to the Yaozhou moulded wares were also made at Linru.

The term 'celadon' used to describe green-glazed stonewares fired in reducing atmosphere appears to be European in origin. It probably derives from the name of a character in the pastoral romance *L'Astrée* by Honoré d'Urfé, published in 1610. The shepherd in this play, named Céladon, appeared on stage in a costume of grey-green. The association is between the colour of the glaze and the colour of the costume.

As on the Ding wares, the first type of decoration to be used on Yaozhou wares was carved and incised. A superb example of this type is the 11th century cylindrical box (**26**). The green Yaozhou glaze is more olive in tone than the 10th century Yue ware examples discussed in the previous chapter, although it too is fired in a reducing atmosphere in the kiln. This olive tone is due, at least in part, to a small quantity of titanium as well as the iron in the glaze, and to the fact that coal was used

27

Pair of small Yaozhou ware bowls with moulded decoration on the inside and incised decoration on the outside. Early 12th century. Diameter 9.7 cm. PDF 296 and 297

as fuel. At its best, as on this box, the Yaozhou glaze is clear and bright, and is somewhat thicker than the Yue glaze. These qualities were skilfully exploited by the Yaozhou decorators to achieve a richness of surface not previously observed on monochrome wares. As can be seen from this box, the carved designs have been cut at an angle so that one side of the cut is vertical, while the other is oblique. This technique was also employed on the Ding wares, but on them the glaze was too thin and too pale for its effect to be exploited to full advantage. On the Yaozhou wares however the glaze takes on a darker colour where it runs into the deep cuts, and shades to a paler green where the glaze is thinner, thus imparting an almost dichromatic effect to the carved decoration. As on Ding wares fine parallel lines have been used to add texture to the petals and leaves of the decoration. The choice of decorative motif on this box is also characteristic of Yaozhou wares at their apogee in the Northern Song period. There is a fluent petal band around the sides of the box, while on top of the slightly domed lid is a skilfully disposed peony scroll, encircled by a narrow band of scrolling leaves. As is characteristic of these pieces, where the clay body is free of glaze and has thus been exposed in the kiln (such as at the foot) it has turned to a warm brown colour.

Although the small conical bowls (**27**) might appear at first sight to have carved decoration, they have in fact been moulded. The use of moulds to produce designs on the inside of bowls and dishes was a technique adopted at the Yaozhou kilns, almost certainly influenced by the Ding potters, in the early 12th century. The decorative schemes employed, however, were quite different from those seen on the white wares. In the case of these two bowls the decoration is nearer to that seen on the carved Yue bowl (16). These Yaozhou bowls have on the interior a design of deeply cut waves with four fishes swimming around the sides and a monster (possibly a giant squid) emerging from the central area; on the outside they are enlivened by incised radiating lines.

Quite a different style of moulded decoration associated with the Yaozhou kilns in the Jin period may be seen on the dish (**28**). The design on this dish is much shallower than that in the bowls. It is

44

not so delicately or so sharply cut as on the Ding moulded bowl (24), but the optical properties of the thicker, darker glaze are still exploited. It does, however, resemble the moulded Ding pieces in having a very crowded appearance. The decoration on the Yaozhou piece is of three bunches of lotus flowers and other plants, with three roundels inter- posed. Each roundel contains a Chinese character, and toge- ther they read 'three bunches of lotus'.

One area of schol- arly research under- taken by Sir Percival David was Ru ware, and his findings are recorded in his remarkable paper, 'A Commentary on Ju Ware', pub- lished in the *Transactions of the Oriental Ceramic Society* in 1937. Ru ware (spelt Ju in the Wade-Giles system of romanization used at that time) is one of the rarest and most treasured of all the 'classic' wares of China. Extant texts indicate that the ware was made for a very short period of time, from around 1086 to 1127, when the Song court was forced to flee south. Chinese archaeologists have recently located and begun excavations at the kiln producing the ware at Qingliangsi, Baofeng county, Henan province. Some of the sherds found there have features in common with the intact examples in the Foundation's collection. With Sir Percival's special interest in the ware he was able to acquire twelve examples of Ru – more than any other col- lection outside China. A number of these pieces are known previously to have been in the Chinese Imperial Collection and bear inscriptions which extol their rarity and value. One such bowl (**29**) with a beauti- ful soft finely crackled blue-grey glaze has the elegantly flared foot characteristic of the ware, and a mouthrim bound with metal. Its body material accords well with the description 'the colour of ashes after burning', used by one of the Chinese archaeologists who excavated the kiln site. On the inside of the bowl is an imperial inscription which may be translated as:

28
Yaozhou ware dish with moulded decoration. 12th century. Diameter 19.7 cm. PDF 245

Jun wares were all produced for the Xiuneisi [Imperial Household
  Department of Works].
Many [old] dishes have survived, but bowls it is difficult to find.
In the Palace alone are stored well-nigh a hundred dishes,
Yet bowls are as rare as stars in the morning.
What is there, indeed, for which a cause cannot be found?
Large bowls are difficult to preserve, small dishes easy.
In this I find a moral and a warning –
The greater the object, the greater the task of caring for it.
Composed by Qianlong in the cyclical year *bing wu* [1786], and inscribed
  by imperial order.

29
Ru ware bowl with metal
bound mouthrim. Early
12th century. Diameter
16.7 cm. PDF 3

Two seal marks, *Bi de* (the measure of virtue) and *Lang run* (clear and unctuous), have also been incised.

It will have been noted that the emperor refers to Jun ware rather than Ru ware, but this is by no means the only time that he expressed admiration for something he failed to identify correctly. The bowl may well have been equally treasured by the previous emperor, however, for a bowl bearing a striking resemblance to this one (even to the extent of the metal band and particular lines of crackle in the glaze) is shown in the *Scroll of Antiquities*, mentioned above, which is dated by its inscription to 1728, the third year of the reign of the emperor Yongzheng.

Most of the Ru pieces are undecorated and rely on the beauty of their glaze and the elegance of their form for their aesthetic appeal. The Foundation does, however, have one exception to this rule in an oval brush-washer (**30**), which has on the inside – barely discernible under the glaze – an impressed design of what may be stylized flowers but are more likely to be fish. Like most other examples the brush-washer is entirely covered with glaze, and has been fired on spurs, leaving small elliptical marks on the base, which the Chinese describe as 'sesamum seed' marks.

Judging from the few examples of Ru ware that have survived to the present day, it seems that these pieces either had very simple elegant forms like the bowl and brush-washer, or forms adopted from metal-work or lacquer. There is an example in the Foundation of a Ru vessel in the form of a *lian* (toilet box), which was a popular bronze and lacquer shape of the Han dynasty. Perhaps even more attractive is the Ru bowl-stand (**31**) which has taken its shape from a prototype in either silver or lacquer. A handleless bowl would have rested on its simple rounded bowl, which is surrounded by a flange formed of foliated overlapping petals. The bowl-stand has a flared footring, but no base.

Another northern ware that is a relative of both Ru and the olive green celadons of Shaanxi and Henan provinces is Jun ware. This was made at kilns spread over a wide area including those at Linru and Yuxian, and enjoyed considerable popularity from the early Song period until well into the Ming dynasty. These pieces, of which the Foundation has a large and varied collection, are classed as stonewares, although not all have in fact been fired to stoneware temperatures. They are generally more heavily potted than the Ru wares, and the sandy marks left on their bases by the lumps of clay on which they were fired are much less neat than the Ru 'sesamum seeds'. It is, nevertheless, an extremely attractive ware, usually undecorated because of its thick opaque glaze, which appears in a range of clear blue tones ranging from sky blue to lavender. The glaze indeed often has an almost opalescent quality due to the effect of light on certain features

30
Ru ware brush-washer with stamped decoration. Early 12th century. Length 14.3 cm. PDF 76

31
Ru ware bowl-stand. Early 12th century. Diameter 16.8 cm. PDF 81

32

Jun ware pillow. 12th
century. Length 29.8 cm.
PDF 2

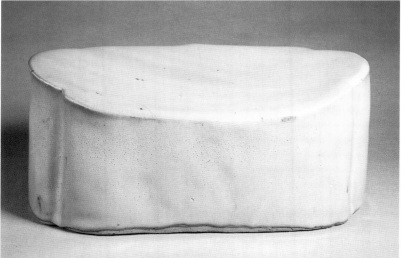

within the glaze: the mass of small gas bubbles trapped in the glaze, the
formation of tiny crystals, and an emulsion formed by two liquids within
the glaze.

The early examples of Jun ware have a plain bluish glaze. One of
these early pieces is the head-rest (**32**). Head-rests appear in a variety
of shapes in Chinese ceramics, and this one is of *ruyi* shape (the shape
of the head of an auspicious sceptre). It bears on its base an interesting
imperial inscription (recorded in *The Collected Works of the Emperor*

Qianlong, Volume 81, Section IV), applied by order of the emperor Qianlong in 1781. The inscription describes the piece as being an example of the legendary Chai ware which was supposed to be 'as blue as the sky, as clear as a mirror, as thin as paper, as resonant as a musical stone'.

In the early 12th century the potters making Jun wares began to add splashes of copper oxide to the unfired glaze. The result, when the pieces were fired in their normal reducing atmosphere, was to produce bright purple areas contrasting with the soft blue tone of the glaze. As can be seen on a rare example of a Jun narrow necked vase (**33**) the effect was very dramatic. The copper splashes were, in the first instance, apparently casually applied. It would not be accurate to say that they were random, for a glance at the vase is enough to tell us that the splashes have been carefully placed for harmonious effect, but they form no specific design. However, there do exist examples, which probably date to the 13th century, where the purple colour has been used to create a recognizable design, such as a head-rest with the Chinese character for 'pillow' painted upon it. A more subtle use of the purple tone was, however, made on a number of vessels in the Foundation's collection to delineate particular areas of a piece. The most usual arrangement is seen on the bulb bowls where the inside is blue and the outside is purple, but one of the most effective is surely that on the slightly lobed box (**34**), the sides of which have been given a delicate mauve blush which gently shades to blue on the top of the lid.

33
Jun ware vase with copper splashes. 12th century. Height 29.1 cm. PDF 92

Although they do not form major parts of the Collection, it is not possible to leave the northern wares of the Song period without reference to two further wares produced at kilns in the north of China: the Cizhou wares and the Henan black-glazed wares.

34
Jun ware box. 12th century. Diameter 11.1 cm. PDF 42

49

Cizhou ceramics were popular rather than 'classic' wares, produced at a great number of kilns over a wide area of north China and employing a considerable range of decorative techniques. The majority of the Cizhou-type wares in the Collection were acquired by Sir Percival David mainly because they bore dated or other interesting inscriptions. The mortuary pillow (**35**) is such a piece, and is, in addition, an example of one of the unusual decorative techniques employed on Cizhou wares. The head-rest part of the pillow is leaf-shaped and stands on a rather high pentagonal column. As is the case with almost all Cizhou wares, the pillow has been given a pale slip over the clay body. On top of the pale slip another slip in brown has been applied. The decoration has been incised through the brown slip to reveal the pale surface below, so that the design of plant scrolls and phoenix stands out in white against the brown ground. Like the majority of Cizhou wares the pillow has been given a thin colourless glaze over the slip decoration. On the unglazed base there is an impressed cartouche with an inscription that may be translated as 'Made by the Zhang family'. The name of this family appears on a number of head-rests (more commonly with painted decoration) from Cixian. A further cartouche appears on the underside of the head-rest itself, which gives a date, 'the third year of Zhihe', equivalent to 1056. This mortuary pillow is thus a rather rare example among early Chinese ceramics, furnishing information on both the potter and the date of manufacture.

35
Cizhou ware mortuary pillow. Dated by inscription to 1056. Width 30.5 cm. PDF 318

The black-glazed wares of north China are closely linked to the Cizhou wares. They were made at a number of the same kiln centres, and not surprisingly have the same wide variety of body types. In contrast to the southern black wares, which will be discussed in the next section, these northern wares usually have rather pale bodies and are therefore given a coating of thick black slip before a transparent brown glaze is applied. Incised or moulded decoration would not be effective on these wares, and so any decorative effects have to be achieved through permutations of slip and glaze colour, and sophisticated adjustments to the firing cycle within the kiln. The Foundation has an especially successful example of the so-called 'oil spot' glaze on a small round-sided tea bowl (**36**). Tiny spots of metallic iron have been caused to precipitate out onto the surface of the glaze, giving the appearance of droplets of oil floating on water. The whole of the clay body has been covered in dark slip, although characteristically the glaze does not reach the footring but stops about three-quarters of the way down the outside of the bowl.

36
Henan black ware bowl with 'oil spot' glaze. 11th-12th century. Diameter 9 cm. PDF 301

The Wares of the Southern Song

1127-1279

There were of course many kilns producing ceramic wares in central and south China during the period preceding the flight of the Song court from its northern capital at Kaifeng to Hangzhou in northern Zhejiang in 1127. We have already mentioned the Yue kilns in an earlier section, and there were other kilns manufacturing a variety of wares. Although the southern kilns increased in number during the 10th century, it was not until the early 12th century that they received the impetus for development that had previously been afforded to the northern kilns by the patronage of the Northern Song court and the wealthy inhabitants of the Song capital at Kaifeng. Following the move of the court to Hangzhou the southern kilns received court patronage and adapted their wares accordingly. With the development of overseas trade through the southern ports a number of kilns also found themselves catering for foreign markets on an unprecedented scale.

Some kilns were of course less affected than others by political events, and among those that probably felt the changes least keenly were the Jian kilns in the mountain valleys of northern Fujian province. These kilns produced a black ware that had some features in common with the Henan black wares discussed in the previous section. It is interesting to note that the popularity of black wares has been linked to a change in fashion in tea drinking. Green tea had looked most appealing in celadon bowls, but when the fashion for whisked tea became prevalent, it was noticed that the white foam on the top of the tea contrasted pleasingly with a dark-glazed ware. The habit of drinking tea had, of course, also become established in the monasteries where it was felt to be an aid to meditation, and the Jian wares being made for local domestic use found their way into the local Chan (Zen) Buddhist monasteries. Japanese monks used to visit these monasteries and thus also became acquainted with these Jian wares which in due course they took back to Japan, where the Chinese wares had a considerable influence on Japanese tea wares.

37
Jian ware tea bowl with 'hare's fur' glaze. 11th-13th century. Diameter 12.2 cm. PDF 303

The tea bowl (**37**) is typical of one of the most popular types of Jian ware. It is made of a rather coarse very dark clay over which has been applied a thick black glaze. The glaze has run down the inside of the bowl to pool in the bottom and formed a thick treacly welt on the outside, about three-fifths of the way down the sides of the bowl. Where it has run the glaze appears streaked and metallic, an effect due to the different colours of the various forms of iron oxide produced in the glaze by control of the kiln atmosphere during firing, and to the separations that took place within the glaze. It is the resemblance of the streaky glaze to hare's fur that gives it its popular name. These wares, and others from the Jizhou kilns which will be discussed below, are also often referred to by their Japanese name, *temmoku* wares. The rim of this bowl has been bound with silver. This rim binding was often done by the Japanese as the running of the glaze away from the rim left the latter slightly rough,

38
Jizhou ware bowl with 'tortoise shell' glaze. 11th-13th century. Diameter 12.8 cm. PDF 306

due to the coarse grain of the clay from which the bowls were made. The silver binding therefore combined visual attractiveness with a more pleasant surface from which to drink.

Another group of kilns producing dark-glazed wares were those in southern Jiangxi province that take their name from the local market town of Jizhou. These kilns made wares using a great variety of decorative techniques, some of which were employed nowhere else in China. The clay body was quite variable in colour and texture. Although vases, ewers and jars were made at these kilns it is nevertheless the bowls that predominate and these include not only the more usual rounded and conical bowls but also lobed examples. One of this latter type with a particularly interesting glaze permutation is the bowl (**38**). This finely potted bowl is basically conical in shape, but has been given five lobes by gentle indentation of the sides. The application of splashes of wood-ash glaze over the black glaze has been used to achieve a mottled effect with a striking resemblance to tortoise shell, an effect further enhanced by the texture of the glaze which has been allowed to become slightly matt, thus emphasizing the colour variations. Like the Jian bowl this Jizhou example has also had its rim bound with silver.

The interest in celadon wares on the part of the Song court and other wealthy segments of society did not come to an end when the products of the northern kilns were no longer available to them, and the establishment of the Southern Song saw increased patronage for those kilns in the south of China producing green wares. The two most important centres for this production were the kilns near Hangzhou, which made Guan wares, and those in Zhejiang and northern Fujian provinces that produced Longquan celadons and also imitations of Guan ware. The Foundation has superb collections of both Guan and Longquan

39
Guan ware bottle vase.
13th century. Height
18 cm. PDF 4

40
Guan ware dish. 12th-
13th century. Diameter
17 cm. PDF A46

wares, going right through the Southern Song and Yuan periods and into the Ming dynasty when the kilns finally waned and production declined irrevocably. Both Guan and Longquan celadon wares were, however, imitated in the Qing dynasty with varying degrees of success, as can be seen from a number of examples in the David Collection.

Guan (official) wares are believed to have been produced in two localities in the Southern Song period. One kiln was said to have been set up under the direction of the Xiuneisi (Imperial Household Department of Works) in the precincts of the palace in Hangzhou. This kiln site has not been excavated and is unlikely to be in the foreseeable future because it is beneath a modern residential area. The other kiln site is at Jiaotanxia, built as the name suggests 'below the Suburban Altar' on the outskirts of Hangzhou, where extensive excavations have been carried out since its discovery in 1930. These kilns appear to have been producing a ware having many features in common with Yue ware before the court moved to Hangzhou. From the mid 12th century, however, the wares from these kilns took on a rather different appearance and became more reminiscent of Ru ware in such features as the neat oval spur marks, the absence of decoration, and the choice of shapes. Guan wares appear in three qualities, depending upon the colour and depth of the glaze, the colour of the clay

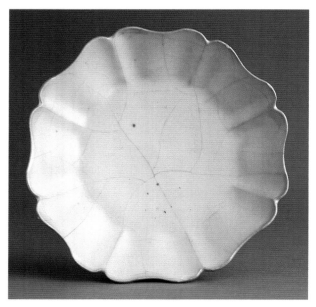

body, and the closeness of the crackle. The highest quality may be seen in a number of examples in the Foundation's collection including the bottle vase (**39**) and the foliated dish (**40**). The exquisite bottle vase has been described by R.L. Hobson as realizing 'all our most extravagant ideas of what Kuan [Guan] ware should be'. The high-fired clay body of this piece is so dark as to be almost black, and is very thin. Its thick blue-grey glaze has almost certainly been applied in several layers, and has a rich lustrous quality. The crackle, which is intentional on Guan wares, is widely spaced and delicately enhances the elegant shape of the vase. The golden brown colouration of the crackle, which follows the stress lines of the thrown shape, derives from iron in the body material rather than being stained from the outside as is the case with many other examples. The widely flaring mouth and slightly flaring foot are both bound with metal. The foliated dish also has the same clear blue-grey glaze and widely spaced crackle as the bottle vase. The shape of this dish with its petal-like foliations and flat base is one that, like the Ru bowl-stand discussed above, is also found in silver and lacquer ware.

At the beginning of the 12th century illustrated catalogues were published of bronzes and jades in the collection of the emperor Huizong, and these marked a revival of interest in antiquarianism that found expression in the archaistic bronze and jade shapes adopted in many of the decorative arts, including the ceramic wares of the Guan and Longquan kilns. One of the bronze shapes most frequently reproduced in ceramics was the *gui*, and there is a fine Guan ware incense burner of such a shape (**41**). The glaze on this piece is not of quite such a clear blue-grey as the previous dish and vase, and its crackle is a good deal closer and darker in colour, giving the piece an altogether less ethereal appearance. The original bronze shape has, nevertheless, been well adapted to the ceramic medium, in that it has been simplified and the piece has no surface decoration, unlike a 14th century example in the Collection which has a design of the eight trigrams moulded under the glaze (PDF 15).

Possibly the most eccentric shape to be adopted in the repertoire of any ceramic ware is the archaic jade *cong* shape, which appears among these Guan archaistic items. The *cong* is basically a cylinder onto

41
Guan ware incense burner. 13th century. Height 9 cm. PDF 16

which have been applied four notched tri-hedrons, giving the piece an almost square section. Numbers of ancient jade *cong* have been found at burial sites, but their purpose has yet to be ascertained. The simplest way of producing this shape in clay was to mould each of the four sides and then lute the four slabs together, adding the top and base separately. The other way was for the potter to throw a cylinder on the wheel and then lute on the four trihedral sections, a method which produced a very heavy piece of ceramic ware. The Guan *cong* (**42**) was produced by the latter method, and unlike some other examples has been given a base so that it could have been used as a vase. This *cong*-shaped vessel has a somewhat paler body than the previous examples and the glaze, although clear and lustrous, has a slightly greener tone. As can be seen in the detail of the *Scroll of Antiquities* (12), this Guan ware *cong*, or a piece remarkably similar to it, was in the emperor Yongzheng's collection, and was obviously regarded as an impe-

42
Guan ware vase. 13th century. Height 18.3 cm. PDF 62

rial treasure in the first half of the 18th century.

A version of Guan ware was also produced at the Longquan kilns of southern Zhejiang and northern Fujian provinces. A considerable number of kiln complexes had grown up in the Longquan area, the largest of which were at Dayao and Jincun, and during the Southern Song period these greatly increased in size. During this period they also changed the style of their products from wares with incised decoration that reflected

43
Longquan ware incense burner. 12th-13th century. Height 9.7 cm. PDF 205

the influence of Yue and Yaozhou to wares more in keeping with the refined, subtle and archaistic tastes of the Southern Song court.

Many connoisseurs have seen in the glaze perfected at the Longquan kilns a deliberate attempt to imitate jade. Certainly the glaze on these southern celadons is quite different from the glossy transparent glaze on the Yaozhou wares of the north. The Longquan celadon glaze, which reached its peak of perfection during the Southern Song, has the bluish-green colour characteristic of the highest quality southern celadons, and is also a thick glaze containing a high percentage of tiny bubbles, which give it a somewhat opaque but almost luminous quality that is reminiscent of jade.

The interest in archaistic forms as well as the superfluousness of decoration under such a glaze can be seen on the *gui*-shaped incense burner (**43**). This elegant piece displays a slightly more angular profile than the previous Guan example, while its rather larger handles retain a shape closer to the bronze prototype than its Guan counterpart (41). Although the clay body of these pieces is almost white, as can be seen where the glaze is thin, the clay has reoxidized to a reddish brown where

44
Pair of Longquan ware funerary urns. 12th-13th century. Height 27 cm. PDF 204 a and b

it has been exposed in the kiln. As we shall see later, this is a characteristic of the Longquan body material that is put to good use by the ceramic decorators of the Yuan period.

The Foundation has a pair of urns (**44**) of a type associated with funerary ritual in the Southern Song. These have ovoid bodies, which have been lightly decorated with overlapping petals that accentuate the low vertical ridges. The shoulders rise in two rounded steps to collars and wide cylindrical necks. The

slightly domed lids are intact, and each lid is surmounted by a short-tailed bird finial. On the shoulder of one urn has been placed a freely modelled tiger, while around the other coils an equally casual dragon. These urns traditionally come in pairs, the white tiger being the symbol of the West and the green dragon the symbol of the East, and were placed in the tomb in positions appropriate to the direction they symbolized.

The vertical ridges and lightly sketched lotus petals seen on the bodies of the urns are also frequently used on the outside of Longquan bowls and dishes. The small dish with a straight flattened rim and plain well (**45**) has this decorative device used around its curved outer sides. The decoration on its flat base is of a type very popular in the Southern Song period. Two fish (already noted as being symbolic of abundance) have been sprig-moulded and then applied to the inside of the bowl with the aid of a sloppy clay mixture. The whole piece has then been glazed and fired so that the fish appear in low relief, their appearance softened by the opacity of the glaze.

45
Longquan ware dish with sprig-moulded decoration. 13th century. Diameter 14.1 cm. PDF 265

Although it is not strictly an imperial ware and thus is not represented in great numbers in the Collection, we should not leave the Southern Song period without mentioning the ware known by the Chinese name *qingbai* (blue white) or *yingqing* (shadow blue), both descriptive of the colour of its glaze. In addition to being a very attractive ware, there were features that emerged during early stages of development of this ware that paved the way for the establishment of underglaze blue decorated wares in the succeeding dynasty.

These *qingbai* wares were made at kilns in the Jingdezhen area of Jiangxi province, a region that was to become and remain to this day the most important porcelain producing area in China. Unlike their European counterparts the Chinese potters found all the raw materials needed for making porcelain close at hand and easy to obtain. Indeed the material known in the west as 'kaolin', and used along with china stone to produce porcelains, takes its name from the Gaoling hills near Jingdezhen whence it was obtained.

Qingbai was a porcelain with a pure white sugary body covered in the case of the finest pieces with a transparent glaze having an icy bluish tinge. Unlike their Northern Song counterparts but like celadons, these southern white wares were fired in a reducing atmosphere which

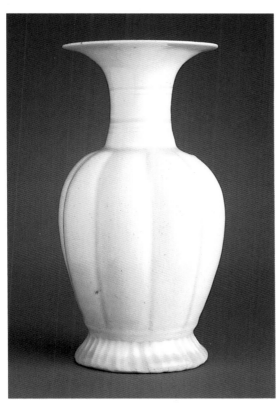

produced their bluish tone. *Qingbai* devoid of surface decoration can be seen at its best on a lobed vase (**46**) which has a shape that was popular in Korean celadon wares of the Koryŏ dynasty (918-1392), and was also seen in silverware. The lobes, horizontal banding and narrow fluting around the foot all serve to provide indentations wherein the blue-toned glaze pools to give areas of clear colour in contrast to the icy white of the rest of the vessel.

46
Qingbai porcelain vase. 11th-12th century. Height 17.5 cm. PDF A496

47
Qingbai porcelain bowl. 12th century. Diameter 13 cm. PDF A459

The conical bowl (**47**) is typical of those produced during the Southern Song dynasty. Unlike the Ding white wares of the north, it has a straight, high footring and was fired standing upright. The sides of the bowl are thinly potted and the glaze has run down the inside to form a clear blue pool in the bottom of the vessel. The blue tinge of the glaze also enhances the cursively incised decoration of floral motifs on the inner walls of the piece, as well as the curvilinear overlapping petals on the outside.

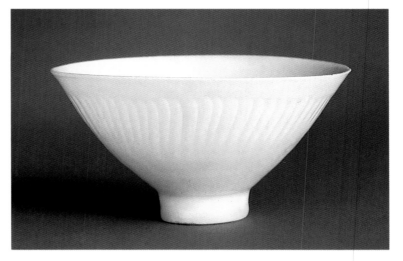

The Wares of the Yuan Dynasty

1279-1368

It is only in fairly recent times that the Yuan dynasty has been recognized as an extremely important period in the development of Chinese ceramics. There had in the past been a tendency to decry the Mongol rulers for exercising no positive artistic influence over the products of the kilns, and for being interested only in the revenue that could be accrued from their sale overseas. While this is not altogether an unjustified criticism, the results of the Mongols' attitude to Chinese ceramic wares were not wholly negative. The influence of the conservative Southern Song court had been a restraining one. A preference had been shown for elegant wares, undecorated or with little or very subtle decoration. Forms were mainly small in size, traditional in shape and with a leaning towards archaism. One of the advantages of Mongol 'barbarian' rule was a freedom from these restraints which made it possible for the potters to experiment. It also allowed into the Chinese kilns influences from outside, and the potters were encouraged to make wares specifically to comply with the tastes of their overseas customers. It is significant that two of the largest collections of high-quality 14th century Chinese ceramics are to be found in the Topkapi Saray, Istanbul, and the Ardebil Shrine, Iran. Maritime trade had been built up under the Song dynasty, not only within East Asia and Southeast Asia, but also with the West. Persian and Arab merchants played a considerable part in this trade and by the Yuan period there were significant numbers of these foreign merchants in China in positions of responsibility. This occurred not least because the Mongols often did not trust the Chinese to work to the benefit of their conquerors. These merchants were thus in a good position to influence the style of wares being produced by the Chinese kilns for export abroad.

In the previous chapter Longquan wares made during the Song dynasty were discussed, but the Foundation also has a fine collection of Yuan dynasty examples, which reflect the spirit of experimentation in this period. A rather rare type of Longquan ware, decorated with iron brown spots, has been much admired by the Japanese and is usually known by its Japanese name *tobi seiji* (spotted green ware). The *tobi seiji* vase in the David Collection (**48**) is of baluster shape with a swelling body and widely flaring mouth. The glaze is of a particularly pleasing opaque soft green with rich dark brown spots. Where the footring is chamfered and clear of glaze it has been burnt to a reddish brown in the kiln, as is typical of these wares.

The tendency of the otherwise very pale grey body to turn reddish brown where exposed in the firing is a feature which was

48
Longquan ware vase of *tobi seiji* type. 14th century. Height 27.2 cm. PDF 217

made use
of by potters
at the Longquan
kilns in the 14th century
in order to produce new decora-
tive effects. The famous large dish in the Collection (**49**) is an especially
fine example of one of these new techniques as well as representing one
of the new large forms that appeared in the 14th century in response to
the requirements of Near Eastern taste. The reawakening of interest in
dramatic surface decoration was also stimulated by the requirements of
foreign markets, but was gradually also assimilated into the products
made for the domestic market. Around the well of this dish a stylized
wave design has been carved into the clay body under the glaze, and it
is apparent that this glaze is less opaque than on the earlier examples and
the underglaze decoration can be seen through it. The rest of the decoration – florets on the flattened rim, and dragon and clouds in the centre

49
Longquan ware dish with
unglazed floated relief
decoration. 14th century.
Diameter 43.1 cm.
PDF 255

– has been produced by sprig-moulding the individual elements and applying them on top of the glaze before firing. Although the piece was fired in a reducing atmosphere like all other celadon wares it was possible to allow a little oxidization during the cooling, after the glaze had stabilized, in order to reoxidize the iron in the exposed body and produce the reddish brown colour which provides so effective a contrast to the soft green of the glaze.

When the glaze was in its liquid state during the firing the sprig-moulded elements were literally floating on the glaze, and thus could only be placed on horizontal surfaces, for otherwise they would slide off. In order to achieve an equivalent decorative effect on a vertical surface, therefore, the Longquan potters devised a different technique. This is well demonstrated on the faceted *meiping* (plum blossom vase) in the Collection (**50**). The vase is octagonal, with the facets continuing up into the neck and down into the foot. Each facet has three panels of moulded decoration. In every case the upper and lower panel has a chrysanthemum spray beneath the glaze. The larger central panels alternate between depictions of another chrysanthemum spray and a sage among clouds. These central panels have been coated with wax before the vase was glazed, to prevent the glaze adhering to those areas. When the piece was fired the glaze matured in the normal way, but the wax burnt off the central panels leaving the clay exposed to biscuit fire to a reddish brown just like the sprig-moulded elements of the previous example. This particular vase, like a number of others of this type, has traces of gold remaining on the biscuit panels, indicating that at one time these were gilded.

50
Longquan ware vase with moulded and reserved decoration. 14th century. Height 24.3 cm. PDF 203

One of the most handsome and important of the Yuan dynasty Longquan wares in the Collection is a large, beautifully proportioned vase with a dated inscription (**51**). The flaring mouth and upper part of the neck are decorated with carved rings. The lower part of the neck and upper part of the body are decorated with a bold floral scroll that has been left in low relief when the background was cut away. The details on the leaves and petals have also been carved and incised under the glaze. The lower part of the body is decorated with carved petals having raised central ridges of a style similar to those seen on the outside of the small dish (45). Around the mouthrim and under

51
Longquan ware temple
vase dated by inscription
to 1327. Height 72 cm.
PDF 237

the glaze has been incised an inscription which may be translated:

> Zhang Jinzheng of the village of Wan'an on Liu [hua] hill at Jingquan in Guacang, a humble believer in the Precious Trinity [of Buddhism], has fired a pair of large flower vases to be placed before the Buddha in the Great Dharma Hall, Juelin temple, with [pledges of] eternal support and prayers that the blessings of good fortune and peace may attend his family. Respectfully inscribed on an auspicious day in the eighth month, *ding mao* (the fourth) year in the Taiding period [1327].

The date inscribed on this vase has recently proved of additional importance, since a vase identical to the one in the Foundation, but having been broken off at the neck, was among the items excavated from the ship that foundered off the Sinan coast of Korea in the 1320s. The date on the Foundation's vase was one of several pieces of evidence which served to confirm the date of the wreck.

Longquan wares of Yuan date are a good deal heavier than those of the preceding Song dynasty, and the thickness of the clay body tended to cause distortion during firing. This vase is one of the pieces in the Collection that displays an ingenious solution to this problem. Most of the base of the vase has been cut away, and a saucer-shaped piece of clay has been placed inside covering the hole. The saucer is held in place not with clay, but with glaze, so that during the firing when the glaze was liquid the saucer could slide on the glaze to accommodate any expansion or contraction of the body.

As was noted earlier, the kilns making Jun wares continued in production into the Yuan period. Like many wares of the Yuan dynasty, those from the Jun kilns became generally larger and heavier in this period, and the bulb bowls, flower pots and flower pot stands characteristic of the 13th and 14th centuries may be included among these. There was frequent use of twin moulds to produce some of the lobed shapes and to achieve a uniformity of size and thickness. The flower pot (**52**) was made by twin moulds, which would have facilitated the forming of the slightly flanged horizontal rim, and the lobing right down through the foot. Like several other examples in the Collection, this piece has a number stamped on the bottom beneath the glaze – in this case the Chinese number *er* (two).

52
Jun ware moulded flower pot. 13th-14th century. Height 19 cm. PDF 33

A study of the numbers *vis-à-vis* the relative sizes of pieces of this type indicates that the numbers do in fact refer to the size. These numbers, together with the fairly small range of shapes produced, are indicative of a considerable degree of standardization at these kilns during this period. The rich purplish tone of most of the glaze on this flower pot is also a characteristic of the increasing use of copper on these later Jun wares, which was used not only for producing splashed effects and shading on the outside of vessels, but also all over some flower pots and stands of this type.

53
Shufu ware bowl with moulded decoration. 14th century. Diameter 12.3 cm. PDF A455

A number of white porcelain wares were manufactured during the Yuan dynasty, as the potters at the Jingdezhen kilns appeared to be experimenting with variations developed from the *qingbai* wares. One of these Yuan white wares is known as *shufu* because the two Chinese characters *shu* and *fu*, which together are usually translated as 'privy council', are frequently incorporated in the underglaze decoration. These *shufu* pieces, like the bowl in the Foundation (**53**), are usually fairly thickly potted, and their glaze has the same bluish tinge seen on *qingbai* wares. The *shufu* glaze, however, is somewhat opaque and slightly matt in contrast to the glossy transparency of the *qingbai* and is often referred to as *luanbai* (egg white). It seems possible that these wares were made for ceremonial use by the Shumiyuan, which was a government ministry dealing with military and civil affairs. There are only two major decorative schemes, in addition to the Chinese characters mentioned above, seen on the inside of bowls and dishes of this type. These are either geese among clouds or, as on the David Collection bowl, a lotus scroll. The design on this bowl has been moulded in low relief and is quite difficult to see owing to the thickness and opacity of the glaze. The shape of the bowl is characteristic of these wares, with a footring quite small in size for the diameter of the bowl, and almost straight sides that form a sharp angle with the base of the vessel and flare towards the mouthrim.

The most significant development of the Yuan period was the extensive use of decoration on porcelain painted under the glaze, particularly that in cobalt blue. In the Tang dynasty cobalt blue was used as a colorant in a lead glaze, both as part of the *sancai* (three colour) palette and also as a monochrome. In both these cases, of course, the body

54
Small plate with applied
decoration. Mid 14th
century. Diameter
15.7 cm. PDF A562

55
The 'David Vases' with
underglaze blue decora-
tion. Dated by inscription
to 1351. Height 63.5 cm.
PDF B613 and B614

material of the wares was earthenware. Recent excavations in China have brought to light some sherds
which appear to be Tang dynasty porcelain
decorated with underglaze cobalt blue.
There have also been several finds of
Song dynasty pieces that incorporated
cobalt blue in their decorative schemes.
It must be said, however, that these
early excavated pieces are extremely
rare, and generally not of unduly high
quality. It is not until the Yuan period
that underglaze blue decoration of a
high standard became established at
the Jingdezhen kilns.

It is perhaps ironic that blue and
white wares, which are linked so inexora-
bly with China in the minds of people of other
nations, should not initially have found much
favour with the Chinese themselves. The cobalt itself
was imported into China – probably from the Kashan area – and the
highly decorative underglaze painted wares were made mainly for
export to the Near East. The influence of these Western markets can be
seen both in the new shapes that were made in porcelain which had their
origins in Near Eastern metalwork and glass, and also in some of the new
decorative motifs that were adopted and incorporated into tightly
packed decorative schemes based on mathematical progressions and an
aesthetic that were quite alien to the Chinese ceramic artist.

Before looking at some of the Foundation's superb early underglaze painted wares, another rare Yuan dynasty piece should be noted.
This small plate is quite finely potted, and has a flat, unglazed base, low
straight sides and a flattened rim (**54**). There is a three-clawed dragon
pursuing a flaming pearl produced in low relief and laid over the blue
pigment. The typically mid 14th century dragon with its thin neck and
small head stands out in white against a rich cobalt blue ground. This
style of decoration was to recur in the Jiajing period in the Ming dynasty,
but on these later pieces the reserved white area is biscuit fired, while the
dragon on the small Yuan dynasty plate is covered with a transparent
glaze having a faint greenish tinge.

The most famous pieces in the Foundation's collection are undoubtedly the so-called 'David Vases' (**55**). These vases have for decades been the most important Chinese blue and white ceramics, serving
as the cornerstones of the chronology for other 14th century pieces. The

reason for their importance is that these vases bear dated inscriptions. As mentioned above, most early blue and white wares were made for export and consequently were not inscribed. These two temple vases not only bear painted decoration of the highest quality but also have long, very similar dedicatory inscriptions on their necks. The one on PDF B613 may be translated as follows:

> The faithful disciple and member of the Jingtang Society, Zhang Wenjin of Dexiao lane in the village of Shunzheng in Yushan district of Xinzhou, is happy to present an altar set of an incense burner and vases as a prayer for the protection of the whole family and for the peace and prosperity of his descendants. Recorded on an auspicious day in the fourth month of the eleventh year of Zhizhen [1351]. Dedicated before the Zingyuan altar of the General Hu Jingyi.

The Jingtang Society would have been a religious society allied to the Buddhist faith. Xinzhou is the area now known as Guangxin and is about 110 kilometres southeast of Jingdezhen. General Hu Jingyi appears to be a local deity who would have been honoured alongside the more universally recognized members of the Buddhist or Daoist pantheon.

The rather complex profiles of these vases almost certainly derive from metalwork, and lend themselves to the banded style of decoration that has been used on them. Happily, from the point of view of their importance in dating other pieces, virtually all the major decorative bands in use at that time are employed on these vases. Around the mouth is a chrysanthemum scroll, and below that the upper part of the neck is painted with a band of overlapping plantain leaves into which the inscription has been set. The lower part of the neck has a phoenix flying among clouds on either side, below which is a spiky lotus scroll. The main decorative area around the widest part of the vases is filled by a sinuous dragon with carefully painted scales and four claws on each foot. The dragons on the vases are painted in the same style but are not identical either in stance or facial expression. A wave band runs around the lower part of the main decorative zone and is also found filling the band immediately below it. On the upper part of the high hollow foot is a peony scroll above panels containing auspicious symbols. Both vases have realistically modelled elephant-head handles from which rings would have been suspended. As is the case on most

56
Small plate with underglaze blue decoration. Early 14th century. Diameter 16.1 cm. PDF B684

ceramic pieces with this type of handle, the rings are now lost. The cobalt blue used on these vases is brilliant and well prepared, and the painting is precise and extremely skilful.

Although these vases dated to 1351 are very important, the Foundation does in fact have a number of underglaze cobalt blue wares without inscriptions but which are datable to the early 14th century. One such piece is the small octagonal lobed dish (**56**). Like the blue plate with reserved white dragon (54), this dish is quite finely potted and has a flat unglazed base. The blue is softer and not quite so brilliant as that on the David Vases, but is nevertheless effectively used and well controlled. The lobes are accentuated by small arrow-shaped motifs painted from the rim towards the centre which gives them a more petal-like appearance. Each petal is ornamented with a segment of classic scroll. The inside of the dish is decorated with a lotus scroll showing both closed profiles and open flowers.

Concurrent with the developments in the use of underglaze cobalt blue during the 14th century were developments in the use of underglaze copper red. Copper red had been used in an almost calligraphic style on the Changsha wares of the 9th century, but its controlled use on porcelain seems to have come into its own during the Yuan period. In the latter half of the 14th century the underglaze cobalt blue and copper red developed along similar lines, and this will be discussed below. However the Foundation is fortunate in having an interesting vase decorated in copper red dating to the first half of the 14th century (**57**). This pear-shaped vase with gracefully flaring mouth has its red decoration restricted to the upper part of the main body area. The details of the decoration have been incised into the body under the glaze and the copper red has been casually applied – also under the glaze – to fill in the background and leave the loose floral

57
Vase with underglaze copper red decoration. First half of 14th century. Height 30.5 cm. PDF B666

58
Wine jar with underglaze red and blue decoration. Early 14th century. Height 33 cm. PDF B66l

scroll in reserve against a red ground.

Another extremely important piece in the Collection is a large wine jar decorated with both cobalt blue and copper red and dating to the early 14th century (**58**). This jar is interesting both for its links with a similar wine jar excavated with the hoard found at Baoding in Hebei province, and also for its links with the so-called Gaignières-Fonthill vase (named after two of its previous owners). The latter vase, now in Dublin, dates to approximately 1300 and is known to have arrived in Europe in the early 14th century. It is a white piece with *qingbai* glaze, decorated with beaded relief and open-work panels similar to those on the David Foundation blue and red jar.

The David blue and red jar is a sturdily potted jar of the shape known in Chinese as a *guan*. It has a flat unglazed base, swelling form and short cylindrical neck. Its thick glaze contains masses of tiny bubbles and has the soft greenish tinge characteristic of these early wares. Around the neck is a simple half-cash design, while on the shoulders is a cloud-collar design of alternating large and small panels. The smaller panels have a single emblem painted within their outline, while the larger ones are filled with many-leafed floral scrolls. Four large panels have been recessed into the main decorative area. These panels are outlined by two rows of beaded relief, glazed but unpainted, while the panels themselves are filled with relief floral elements decorated in underglaze cobalt blue and copper red. Between the lower areas of the panels are tricorn motifs of scrolling tendrils. Below these are petal panels which reach the foot of the jar, each containing a pendent scrolling device.

The Wares of the Ming Dynasty

1368-1644

The period that saw the end of the Yuan dynasty and the re-establishment of a native Chinese dynasty – the Ming – was a very difficult one for the area around Jingdezhen. A good deal of the fighting took place in Jiangxi province, and even after the end of the dynastic wars, the area suffered both from uprisings and punitive expeditions against local rebellions. Indeed it seems very likely that the kilns closed down for a short time. The closure of ports and general disruption of trade also had a significant effect on the ceramic industry. On the one hand they necessitated a greater concentration on products that would appeal to the home market, and on the other they almost certainly interrupted the supply of cobalt coming into China from the Near East.

The disruption of the supply of cobalt is attested to by the brief predominance of underglaze copper red wares over those decorated in cobalt blue. As has been mentioned, these two decorative colours developed side by side, but the potters found the copper even more difficult to control than the cobalt and generally less satisfactory. For a short period at the end of the 14th century, however, more red decorated wares were made than blue.

A very fine example of one of these late 14th century underglaze copper red wares in the David Foundation is the boldly decorated ewer (**59**). Here we can see that the potter has almost entirely overcome one of the main problems of these wares, that of the red turning pale silver-grey in the firing. The very complex style of decoration is typical of ewers made in the late 14th century. It is worth noting that these pear-shaped ewers are identical to the pear-shaped vases except for the addition of spout and handle, and their decorative schemes are therefore similar. The tops of the handle, spout and mouth of the vessel are all the same height, giving the piece a pleasing balance, and the long spout is stabilized by being attached to the neck with a cloud-shaped strut. The small ring on the top of the handle could have been used to attach the lid which is now lost. A narrow key-fret

59
Ewer with underglaze red decoration. Late 14th century. Height 32.5 cm. PDF A696

band runs around the mouth of the ewer, while on the neck are a band of plantain leaves with white central veins and heavy outlines, a larger key-fret band, and a band of knobbed classic scrolls. On the shoulder is a plain, reduced version of the cloud-collar, below which is a well drawn variegated floral scroll. On the lower part of the body are petal panels leading down to the foot, which is decorated with a classic scroll. The spout and handle are decorated with mixtures of floral scrolls, classic scrolls and key-fret bands. In some areas, such as that around the base of the spout, these bands demarcate the joins which would have been visible on the original metalwork ewer from which the ceramic vessel derives its shape.

With the return of peace and the reopening of trade routes, cobalt

60
Large flask with under-glaze blue decoration. Early 15th century. Height 43.8 cm. PDF 662

once more became available to the ceramic decorators and the Near Eastern markets were once again the recipients of fine Chinese ceramics. Two magnificent flasks in the Foundation's collection represent the finest of the larger-sized wares produced at the beginning of the 15th century. One flask (PDF B667), decorated with a blue dragon against a background of floral scrolls, has an exact counterpart in the Topkapi Saray in Istanbul where it has been given a silver mouth mount and domed lid. The other large flask in the Foundation is even more spectacular (**60**). It has a heavy, but well potted, flattened globular shape with a slightly flaring neck, and stands on a low foot with a glazed base. Around the neck is a band of knobbed classic scrolls and another of lotus scrolls. It is, however, in the dramatic decoration around the main body of the vessel that the impact of the piece lies. On each side of the flask a lively three-clawed dragon is incised into the body under the glaze. The dragons are reserved in white against a background of waves painted in cobalt blue. The painting of these waves is in a particularly strong and fluent style that is characteristic of the early 15th century.

61
Flask with underglaze blue decoration. Early 15th century. Height 30.8 cm. PDF A612

In contrast to the lively painting on this large flask, a more refined style may be seen on a smaller flask of similar, or marginally later, date (**61**). 'Precious moon flask' is the name by which the Chinese usually call a vessel of this type, and although it is now associated with China, the shape in fact derives from one found in Syrian glass. As with the larger flask, this piece has a flattened globular form with slightly flaring short neck, which in this case is supported on either side by two small cloud-shaped handles. The vessel has no footrim, but a flat unglazed base. A spray of bamboo adorns either side of the neck, while at both shoulder and base are bands of detached scrolling cloud motifs. The decoration of the main area has been painted with considerable skill. On one side there is a bird on a prunus branch and a bamboo spray, while on the other is a bird on a peach branch and a bamboo spray. This exquisitely painted piece had been damaged at some time, but so much was it valued by one of its previous owners that it has been lovingly restored and the infill given a gold lacquer finish typical of Japanese repairs of the highest quality.

It is extremely difficult to be precise about the dating of early 15th century blue and white wares, but they are generally characterized by a vitality in their painting style, the so-called 'orange-peel' effect on the surface of the thick glaze where tiny bubbles have burst and left minute indentations, and what is known as the 'heaped and piled' effect caused by different concentrations of cobalt blue within the painted decoration. Chinese ceramic decorators appear to have begun using native cobalt in the 1420s, but its inclusion does not seem to have affected painting style. Some pieces in the Foundation's collection may, with reasonable confidence, be ascribed to the Yongle period (1403-24), although Yongle reign marks are very rare. With the Xuande period, however, came very active imperial interest in the ceramic industry and the placement of large orders for the palace. Existing records state that at one time fifty-eight kilns were producing wares for the court under the supervision of officials appointed from the capital, and it was during the Xuande reign that *nianhao* (reign marks) began to appear regularly on official wares. At this time the reign marks were written in various places on the vessels, such as on the shoulder, on the base, in the centre of bowls, and just below the mouthrim.

62
Large bowl with underglaze blue decoration. Xuande mark and period (1426-35). Diameter 29.5 cm. PDF B619

It is in this last position that the reign mark has been written on a heavy, straight rimmed bowl in the David Collection (**62**). The mark reads *Da Ming Xuande nian zhi* (Made in the Xuande reign of the Great Ming [dynasty]). There are a number of heavily, but extremely precisely potted bowls dating to the Xuande period. Some are fairly shallow, like this example, and some rather deeper but still with a straight rim. The bowls stand on sturdy well-cut footrims and the bases are glazed. Many examples of both types are undecorated on the inside. This bowl is

decorated with a design that became increasingly popular in the first half of the 15th century and remained a favourite motif on all the Chinese decorative arts. The design is of pine, bamboo and prunus, known as the 'three friends of winter', which are also taken to be symbolic of the qualities of a gentleman, and of Confucianism, Daoism and Buddhism. Here the depiction is simple, with the plants accompanied by an ornamental rock of the type admired by Chinese gardeners and painted in naturalistic style up the sides of the bowl. Beneath them is a band of lotus panels and around the foot is a fluent, but somewhat stylized, wave band.

The skills of the Chinese potter were not, however, reserved solely for the making of impressive vessels of the type described above. In the David Collection there are a number of items made with the pastimes of the gentleman-scholar in mind. We will consider those pieces made for use by the scholar at his desk a little later, but another rather charming object in the Foundation also bears a Xuande reign mark and shares with its grander fellows the decorative schemes typical of the period. This little bird seed trough is only 8.8 cm long (**63**). It is made in elongated barrel form with an opening along the upper edge, and two small rings that could be used to tie the feeder to the bars of a songbird's cage. At each end of the trough is a floral medallion, and the sides are decorated with floral scrolls. The reign mark is written within a panel on the side opposite the handles. It has long been the custom to keep songbirds in China, and even today, when the weather is fine their cages are hung in trees to give the birds fresh air, or their owners take them out for a walk, gently swinging the cages to give their occupants a little exercise.

The Xuande period is generally agreed to be the apogee in the development of blue and white porcelain wares, and the Foundation is fortunate to have a particularly fine selection of pieces of this period. Perhaps none demonstrates

63
Bird seed trough with underglaze blue decoration. Xuande mark and period (1426-35). Length 8.8 cm. PDF B693

64
Dish with underglaze blue decoration. Xuande mark and period (1426-35). Diameter 17.8 cm. PDF B679

the skill of the ceramic decorator better than the finely potted dish with slightly everted rim (**64**). In the central field on the inside of the dish a writhing dragon has been painted. It is executed with great vitality in deep blue, the decorator making full use of all the tonal variations at his command. The dragon is shown against a delicately painted background of pale blue waves which provide an effective contrast to the style of the creature itself. In the cavetto two dragons painted in slip are barely visible. This type of decoration is known as *anhua* (secret decoration). On the outside of the dish two more blue dragons chase each other among rocks and clouds. The six-character mark of Xuande is written on the base inside a double ring.

A similar use of contrasting styles on a single piece can also be seen on a finely potted stem cup that, although it bears no reign mark, can be fairly securely dated to the Xuande period. The piece is also of interest in that it combines the use of underglaze cobalt blue with underglaze copper red, and it may be noted that by this time the red is as firmly under the potter's control as the blue (**65**). Like the previous dish, this delicate stem cup with its slightly everted rim also has two dragons painted in slip in *anhua* technique on the inside. On the outside both the cup and its stem have dragons incised into the body under the glaze. A wash of copper red has been applied which has run into the incised lines, highlighting them. The copper has, however, been allowed to soften the edges of the design, with the result that whereas the main area is a clear red, these edges are tinged with green in the way that was to be used to such good effect in the 'peach bloom' glazed wares of the Qing period (see page 94). In contrast to the soft wash of the red dragons, the background against which they stand is a boldly painted depiction of breaking waves, which again display all the tonal qualities of Xuande underglaze blue painting.

65
Stem cup with underglaze blue and red decoration. Early 15th century. Height 10.5 cm. PDF A626

After the exuberance of the Xuande period, the next major reign period, that of the Chenghua emperor, provided ceramic wares with quite different characteristics and an emphasis on refinement and delicacy. These wares are also well represented in the Foundation, one of the finest examples being the dish (**66**). It is finely potted, with an exceptionally white body, and has a gently everted rim. The glaze is thinner and clearer than the Xuande examples, and does not exhibit the 'orange-peel' effect of the earlier period. The decoration both inside and outside the dish is of a lotus scroll with the eight Buddhist emblems (the *chakra*, conch shell, umbrella, canopy, lotus, vase, twin fish and endless knot). The motifs are all carefully outlined and then neatly filled in with even washes of soft clear blue. The cobalt on this dish is without any hint of the 'heaped and piled' effect of the previous pieces, and the painting generally has a refined, elegant quality.

These features are seen even more clearly on the bowl (**67**). This bowl is representative of a type of very fine quality wares decorated with large-scale floral scrolling designs, which are often referred to as 'palace bowls' because of their refined style. Once again the purity of the body

66
Dish with underglaze blue decoration. Chenghua mark and period (1465-87). Diameter 19.2 cm. PDF B627

material is evident, especially since the large areas of background have been left undecorated in order to draw attention to the design of scrolling flower stems. This design appears to depict hibiscus and, as on the previous dish, the outlines have been carefully painted and filled with soft blue wash. On the inside of the bowl in the centre is a single flower medallion. Like many 'palace bowls', this one has no subsidiary decorative bands, only plain fine blue lines at rim and foot. The six-character mark of Chenghua appears on the base inside a double ring.

The elegance of the Chenghua wares continued, to an extent, on to the wares of the Hongzhi period. The painting style of the latter may, however, be considered a little less fluent, as can be seen through a

67
Bowl with underglaze blue decoration. Chenghua mark and period (1465-87). Diameter 14.6 cm. PDF A646

77

comparison of pieces in the Collection dating to these two reign periods. Dated pieces of the Hongzhi period are very rare. There is, however one important dated Hongzhi vase in the Collection (PDF 680) which, although it is not of the same high quality as most of the other blue and white pieces, is nevertheless very significant since it has an inscription dating it to 1496.

Major changes can be observed in the wares of the succeeding Zhengde period, and two quite distinct types of blue and white ware from this reign are represented in the David Foundation. Both types bear reign marks, but while one group has six-character marks, the other has only four characters. The group with the four-character marks is, on the whole, quite small and the pieces somewhat over-decorated. The spittoon or leys jar (**68**) is a good example of this type. It has a widely flaring mouth, the neck rising from a globular body, and stands on a slightly splayed foot. The outside is decorated with four five-clawed dragons perambulating through a rather crowded background of lotus scrolls. At the foot there is a band of small lappets, and on the inside of the flaring mouth two more dragons are painted, also against a background of lotus scrolls. The four-character mark is written on the base inside a double ring.

Most of the pieces in the other category of blue and white wares of the Zhengde period bearing a six-character reign mark are items made for the scholar's desk, and they are usually of very high quality. Most examples are decorated with a motif known as 'Mohammadan scrolls' of the type that can be seen on the particularly fine table screen (**69**). This rectangular screen has these 'Mohammadan scrolls' in the area around the circular cartouche into which the square inscription panel is set. The inscription is well written in Arabic, and accurately reproduces a passage from the Qur'an (Koran). The text is taken from Surat al Jinn, LXXII, v. 18-20. Many of the pieces of this type carry Arabic or Persian inscriptions, and it is thought that they may have been made for the Moslem eunuchs who were very powerful at court during this period. Indeed, when the Imperial Factory was rebuilt during the Zhengde period it was put under

68
Spittoon or leys jar with underglaze blue decoration. Zhengde mark and period (1506-21). Height 15.5 cm. PDF A682

the direct supervision of one of the palace eunuchs, as had been the case in earlier reign periods.

During the Jiajing period large orders were received from the court by the Jingdezhen potteries, and the supervision of the imperial wares was transferred from the palace eunuchs to an official of the prefecture.

69
Table screen with under-glaze blue decoration. Zhengde mark and period (1506-21). Height 45.8 cm.
PDF B687

70
Ewer with underglaze
blue decoration. Jiajing
mark and period (1522-
66). Height 29.2 cm.
PDF B617

This period was one during which there was a rekindling of the artistic vitality in the decoration of blue and white porcelain. The new energy in the painting style on these pieces was also enhanced by the particularly jewel-like blue achieved in the cobalt itself. The ewer (**70**) exemplifies both these features. It is of flattened ovoid form, and on either side there is a slightly raised, leaf-shaped panel with a lively scene of children playing. On one side the children are playing with a hobby horse, and on the other riding a goat. The depiction of children playing is popular on blue and white porcelains of the Jiajing period and may be linked to a Daoist theme of the old regaining their youth. Certainly the Jiajing emperor was much interested in Daoism. On the domed lid of the ewer and on either side of the leaf-shaped panels are flowering and fruiting sprays. A chevron design has been used around the top of the mouth and the edge of the lid, while the handle and rectangular sectioned spout are both decorated with scrolls. At the base of the spout, instead of the usual blue on white scheme, the scrolls have been painted in pale blue against a background of darker blue. There is a six-character mark of Jiajing on the base.

Examples of porcelain with genuine reign marks of the Longqing period are rare, which is not surprising since following a number of disasters (including fire and flood) the official factory making imperial wares was only re-established in 1572. There are, however, several pieces bearing genuine Longqing reign marks in the David Foundation. The cobalt blue of these pieces is almost as jewel-like as that seen on the Jiajing ewer, and has a similar violet tinge to the rich blue. Certain similarities of style can also be seen if the ewer is compared with a little

Longqing box (**71**). Each of the box's seven lobes is decorated, both on the base and on the lid, with flowering and fruiting sprays painted, as on the ewer, with very dark outlines which have then been filled with a wash of deep blue. Like the leaf-shaped panel on the previ-

71
Box with underglaze blue decoration. Longqing mark and period (1567-72). Diameter 12.4 cm. PDF A656

ous piece, the flower-shaped panel on the top of the lid of the Longqing box is also slightly raised. The decoration inside the panel is of a five-clawed dragon painted full face and surrounded by clouds. The edge of both base and cover has a band of classic scrolls. The footrim is lobed like the rest of the box, and on the base a six-character mark is written in particularly good calligraphy.

Also bearing a six-character mark of Longqing on its base is a bowl with an interesting decorative scheme (**72**). In a circular panel on the bottom of the inside of the bowl, a woman and child are shown on a terrace; around the inside of the mouthrim is a peony scroll. On the outside of the bowl, however, the piece is decorated with a calligraphic inscription written in *caoshu* (grass or cursive script), each of the characters carefully outlined in very dark blue before being meticulously filled with a deep blue wash. The inscription is a poem which may be translated:

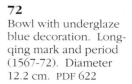

72
Bowl with underglaze blue decoration. Longqing mark and period (1567-72). Diameter 12.2 cm. PDF 622

> The moon shines through the windows at
>   the front of the storeyed house,
> The pretty girls continue to dance and sing.
> The nightjar does not cease to sing until the
>   fourth watch of the night;
> Take heed lest the silk worms do not have
>   enough leaves to eat.

The reign of Wanli was the last of the great periods of ceramic production of the Ming dynasty. In the first year of the reign it was decreed that one of the vice-prefects of Raozhou prefecture should be installed permanently at Jingdezhen to supervise the

73
Writing brush with porcelain handle decorated with underglaze blue. Wanli mark and period (1573-1620). Length 30.5 cm. PDF 627

factory making imperial wares. The size of orders from the court was on occasion so excessive that the potteries were extremely hard pressed to fill them, and one of the supervising censors sent a memorial to the throne in 1583 asking that the court orders be curtailed especially in regard to those categories of wares felt to be unnecessarily extravagant. The David Collection has a number of blue and white wares of the Wanli period, including some of the types of object specifically named as extravagant by the complaining censor. The writing brush with porcelain handle (**73**) is one of these. The widest part of the brush is decorated with two ogival panels each containing a blue dragon amongst clouds. The panels are set against a background of scrolling devices outlined in dark blue and reserved in white against a mid blue ground. Below the bulbous area is a scrolling band, which is also reserved in white, as is the chrysanthemum, lotus and peony scroll which covers the middle section. The six-character reign mark of Wanli is written in blue around the handle. A narrow band of plantain leaves with white reserved outlines encircles the end of the handle. The knob is decorated with a blue rosette and white flowers reserved against a blue ground. All the painting on this brush handle is precise, and beautifully executed in a clear cobalt blue.

A bowl (one of a set) in the Foundation's collection (**74**) combines fine painting in cobalt blue with another decorative technique which was regarded by the censor as being too labour intensive. The sides of this bowl are

74
Bowl with pierced work and underglaze blue decoration. Wanli mark and period (1573-1620). Diameter 8.8 cm. PDF B622

decorated with a particularly delicate pierced lattice. This work is called by the Chinese *linglong* (exquisitely wrought) or *guigong* (devil's work), and the fine tracery was cut into the porcelain when it was leather hard. The lattice is supported by four roundels in the sides of the bowl that have been left solid, and have been painted in cobalt blue with phoenixes surrounded by a scrolling band. Between these roundels are four tricorn pendent panels decorated in underglaze blue, but with a pierced character in white in the centre of each. The characters are *fu shou kang ning*, which translate as 'happiness, long life and tranquillity'. Just below the mouthrim is a delicately painted scrolling band, while a bolder floral scroll appears above the footring, which is decorated with a classic scroll, and has been bound in silver. It is probable that the mouthrim also had a silver band at one time.

Because of China's long history of fine ceramic production it is easy to take for granted the remarkable quality of her porcelains, and to forget just how far she had outstripped her Western trading partners in this field. Various items in the Collection serve to remind us of the esteem in which Chinese porcelains were held

75
Bowl with underglaze blue decoration and semi-precious stones applied to the outside. 16th century. Diameter 12 cm.
PDF A793

in other countries. One of a pair of bowls is (**75**) and shows the kind of extravagant attention that was sometimes lavished on Chinese porcelain in the Near East. This bowl is decorated on the inside with a floral border below the rim, and a design of heron among lotus plants in the central circular panel. All the internal decoration is in underglaze cobalt blue. There are four characters written in underglaze blue on the base of the bowl, which read *fu shou kang ning*, the same auspicious phrase as appeared in the pierced work on the previous bowl. On the outside of the bowl a red overglaze line has been drawn just below the rim and around the foot. The bowl has, however, been further embellished probably by a Turkish owner, who so greatly prized this bowl and its fellow that he has had a design made up of semi-precious stones set in silver and gold applied to their outer surfaces. An even more important clue to the value put upon these Chinese porcelains by their owners in

76

The 'Lennard Cup' with underglaze blue decoration and Elizabethan silver gilt mounts dated by hallmark to 1569-70. 16th century. Diameter 11.9 cm. PDF 695

the West is to be found in another bowl in the Foundation (**76**) which is known as the 'Lennard Cup' after its former owner Samuel Lennard (1553-1618). The outside of the bowl is white, with a lotus scroll incised into the body under the glaze. The inside of the bowl is decorated with a lattice band in underglaze blue just below the rim and a circular panel in the bottom of the bowl with a design of a white hare reserved against a blue rock with pine tree and bamboo. On the base the characters *chang ming fu gui* (long life, riches and honours) are written in underglaze blue. It is a perfectly competently made little bowl, but unexceptional by Chinese standards. The impact of this porcelain bowl on its Elizabethan owner can, however, be judged by the magnificent silver gilt mounts that were applied to the foot and mouth with a cover being made to match. The workmanship is of a very high standard and the mounts bear hallmarks which identify a London goldsmith and date them to 1569-70.

77

Jar with *doucai* decoration. Chenghua mark and period (1465-87). Height 7.4 cm. PDF 797

In addition to the variety of blue and white wares produced in the Ming dynasty, from the 15th century onwards there was increasing interest in the use of colour to produce not only a wider range of monochrome wares, but also a whole range of polychrome wares employing new or adapted techniques. One of these new polychrome techniques is known as *doucai* (dovetailing or contending colours). On these wares the outlines of the design were painted onto the unfired body of the piece in cobalt blue before it was glazed and fired to porcelain temperature. After the piece had come out of the kiln and cooled, overglaze enamel colours were applied within the outlines of the design, and it was fired again at a lower temperature in a muffle kiln. The wares made by this method of decoration are usually rather small and appealed to the refined tastes of the court. The Foundation has a number of such pieces dating to the Chenghua period, when they were at the height of perfection. A small globular jar (**77**) is possibly the most famous of these. The jar is decorated with a design of flowers, butterflies and ornamental rocks in aubergine, red, yellow and green enamels. The plants and rocks grow from or stand upon an undulating blue ground. On the wide flat base of the jar a six-character mark of Chenghua has been written in underglaze blue. Another example of an object decorated in *doucai* style which typifies the delicacy and refinement of these wares is the beautiful little stem cup (**78**). This finely potted piece with its gently curving sides and slightly everted rim stands on a tall stem that flares out towards the foot. Within the underglaze blue outlines green, aubergine and yellow enamels have been used to colour the design of an encircling grape vine. Inside the stem a six-character mark of Chenghua has been written in underglaze blue.

Few *doucai* pieces were made after the end of the Chenghua period, but the ware was much copied in the Qing dynasty. Perhaps the most frequently copied objects were the so-called 'chicken cups', which are referred to in Chinese texts as wedding cups. The Foundation is fortunate in having a genuine Chenghua 'chicken cup' with a Chenghua mark on the base, as well as an excellent copy made in the Kangxi period. Although many of the later copies have spurious reign marks, the example in the David Foundation has a correct Kangxi mark. The similarity between the Chenghua and the Kangxi 'chicken cups' is remarkable, as can be seen when they are placed side by side (**79**). The decorative schemes used on the two cups are identical, but closer

78
Stem cup with *doucai* decoration. Chenghua mark and period (1465-87). Height 8 cm. PDF A779

79
Two 'chicken cups' with *doucai* decoration. The one on the left is Chenghua mark and period (1465-87), the one on the right is Kangxi mark and period (1662-1722). Diameters 8.3 cm and 8.2 cm. PDF A748 and A749

examination reveals that the underglaze blue outlines on the Chenghua example are softer, the drawing is more fluent and the decoration a little better spaced. It is also possible to see that the glaze on the later example is completely colourless compared to the Chenghua glaze which has a very slight greenish tinge.

These *doucai* pieces were very costly to produce, and an equally colourful effect could be achieved using a slightly different technique. Wares produced in this way are known as *wucai* (five colour) wares. The technique works along the same principles as *doucai*, but instead of the outlines being in underglaze blue, which had to be drawn very precisely with no margin for error, whole elements within the design were painted in underglaze blue. A particularly fine example of the *wucai* technique used on a large scale can be seen on the fish bowl (**80**). This massive bowl, which has a six-character mark of Longqing in underglaze blue inside the rim, is decorated with a design of ducks and herons among aquatic plants. As well as the underglaze blue elements, overglaze green,

80
Fish bowl with *wucai* decoration. Longqing mark and period (1567-72). Diameter 55.2 cm. PDF 778

red, yellow and brown have been used. In the case of *wucai* the outlines for the overglaze elements are also painted over the glaze in either black or red. On a smaller scale a dish in the Collection demonstrates the brilliance that could be achieved using this technique (**81**). This dish, which is one of a pair, has a six-character mark of Jiajing on the base in underglaze cobalt blue. On both the inside and the outside of the bowl is a design of golden carp among water weeds. Again there are specific underglaze blue elements within the design, but the main decorative motifs are in fact painted in overglaze enamels. The brilliant yellow of the carp with its red outlines is particularly striking.

81

Dish with *wucai* decoration. Jiajing mark and period (1522-66). Diameter 17.3 cm. PDF A731

Another dish decorated in *wucai* style treats a subject that had become increasingly popular – that of the Dragon Boat Festival (**82**). This festival takes place on the fifth day of the fifth lunar month when the dragon boats race against each other, the dragon being seen as controlling the rains and thus the success of the crops. On the outside of the dish are the four creatures known as the 'four poisons' (the snake, the lizard, the centipede and the scorpion), probably placed there because of the Chinese belief that one counteracts poison with poison. The designs on the inside and outside of the dish are formed of underglaze blue elements in combination with overglaze green, yellow, red and black enamels. On the base a Wanli mark of six characters has

82

Dish with *wucai* decoration. Wanli mark and period (1573-1620). Diameter 20.7 cm. PDF 750

87

83
Dish with overglaze
enamel decoration.
Chenghua mark and
period (1465-87). Dia-
meter 21.7 cm. PDF A763

been written in underglaze blue.

During the Ming dynasty some very fine porcelains were produced decorated only in overglaze enamels with no underglaze blue elements incorporated into the design. A dish in the Foundation's collection (**83**) shows the colour scheme that is most frequently used on these wares. The central area of this dish has a design of two mandarin ducks on a lotus pond. This motif had been popular since the Song dynasty (see 21), and the two ducks are seen as symbolizing marital harmony. In the cavetto of the dish carp swim among lotus plants, while on the outside there is a formal lotus scroll. The two colours that predominate in this palette are green and red, but yellow and turquoise are also used, with just a little black being employed for outlines and details. A six-character Chenghua mark in underglaze blue appears on the base of the dish.

There is a group of wares, most of them dating to the Hongzhi and Zhengde periods, that is decorated with green dragons. Among these pieces dishes are more common than bowls; both forms are well represented in the David Collection, and the bowl (**84**) is a good example. On these wares the outlines and scales of the dragons, which writhe on the inside and perambulate around the outside of the vessels, are incised into the unfired porcelain body. That part of the bowl is painted with wax, which prevents the glaze from adhering to the

84
Bowl with enamel decora-
tion on biscuit. Zhengde
mark and period (1506-
21). Diameter 18.4 cm.
PDF 717

area when the piece is dipped in the liquid glaze. During the firing the wax burns off leaving the dragon in biscuit.

The green enamel is applied over the white biscuit fired area and because there is no glaze, the enamel is able to run into the incised lines, creating a greater density of colour and making the outlines and details more vivid. Details such as the dragon's claws and the tendrils extending from its elbows are painted in enamel over the glaze. The piece could then be fired again at a lower temperature, which was necessary since the overglaze enamels could not be fired at the high temperature needed to produce porcelain. This green dragon bowl has a six-character mark of Zhengde in underglaze blue on its base.

The use of coloured enamels applied to biscuit fired porcelain was employed to even more colourful effect when applied to cover the whole piece, and was especially effective on the wares known as *fahua*. The technique bears a certain resemblance to that used to produce cloisonné enamel wares, and the term *fahua* may be interpreted as 'ware with cloisonné enamel-style decoration'. The decorative motifs are outlined and have some of their details defined by thin lines of slip that stand in low relief on the surface of the vessel. These relief lines serve to contain the different colours within the design. The *guan* jar (**85**) is a good example of the colours and decorative schemes used on these *fahua* pieces. The background colour is cobalt blue, which with turquoise is the most usual background colour, and the designs are in yellow, white and turquoise. On other examples aubergine purple and green are also seen. Around the neck of the jar are small multicoloured clouds, while at its base is a band of *ruyi* heads. On the shoulder is a cloud collar with flowering and fruiting sprays. Jewels hang from strings of beads between the elements of the cloud collar, in a style that began to appear towards the end of the 15th century. The broad central band has a design of peacocks among peonies and rocks depicted on quite a large scale, and around the lower part of the jar is a band of petal panels. This jar dates to about 1500.

The renewed interest in colour in the 15th century also resulted in the production of a wider range of monochrome wares. A very rare 15th century *guan* jar with a turquoise glaze is among

85
Wine jar with *fahua* decoration. *c.* 1500. Height 34.5 cm. PDF 759

those in the David Collection (**86**). Like most of the new monochrome colours, the turquoise glaze could not be fired to the high temperature needed for porcelain and so had to be applied either to an already glazed piece, or one that had been biscuit fired. Most of the other low firing glaze and enamel colours are lead fluxed, but the turquoise is an alkali glaze. The large *guan* jar, which was formerly in the Imperial Collection in Beijing, has an inscription in relief characters on the shoulder. These read *Neifu gongyong* (For use in the Inner Palace). There is a gilt copper band around the neck of the jar.

Sir Percival David acquired a particularly fine collection of monochrome yellow wares of both the Ming and Qing dynasties. One of the earliest of these in the Collection is a dish with a six-character reign mark of Chenghua in underglaze blue on its base (**87**). The yellow enamel on this dish, which has rounded sides and a slightly everted rim, has been applied over a normal colourless porcelain glaze, with the exception of the base which has been left white.

Not all the monochromes of the 15th century had to be refired at a lower temperature. Monochrome copper red wares had been made as early as the late 14th century (see PDF 593), and the copper oxide could be fired to porcelain temperature. The quality of the colour on the late 14th century examples tended to be unstable, and it was not until the 15th century that the deep rich red colour was

86
Wine jar with turquoise glaze. 15th century. Height 33.5 cm. PDF 518

87
Dish with yellow enamel over glaze. Chenghua mark and period (1465-87). Diameter 20.1 cm. PDF A515

90

obtained. One such piece in the Collection is a bowl with a Xuande mark of six characters on the base in underglaze cobalt blue (**88**). It has rounded sides and flaring rim, and has a rich copper red glaze inside and out, but not on the base, which is white. The bowl has a white mouthrim characteristic of these 15th century red monochrome wares.

88
Bowl with copper red glaze. Xuande mark and period (1465-87). Diameter 18.7 cm. PDF A529

Although the early celadon wares had pale grey stoneware bodies, the Jingdezhen potters succeeded in applying a celadon-type glaze to a pure white porcelain body. The effect achieved was quite different from the Song and Yuan celadon wares, but had a new delicacy and clarity, if not the depth of the earlier examples. The bowl illustrated (**89**) is a fine example of such a piece made in the late 15th century. It is well potted with steep sides and a straight mouthrim. A design of scrolling peonies is incised under the glaze on the outside of the bowl, but the inside has been left plain.

During the 16th century, particularly during the Jiajing reign, a variant of the monochrome wares was produced that found particular favour among Japanese patrons. These wares are known by their Japanese name *kinrande* (gold brocade), and have gold decoration applied to the surface of the glaze. The most usual design was one of floral scrolls, which were simply applied to the vessels with a light adhesive and then burnished. Consequently the gold decoration tended to rub off easily. These gold brocade designs were applied to blue, overglaze iron red and green items, bowls being the most usual shape decorated in this way.

A few pieces have survived on which these gold brocade designs have been applied to other colours, and two bowls in the David Foundation are rare examples of the

89
Bowl with incised decoration under a celadon-type glaze. Late 15th century. Diameter 16.5 cm. PDF B566

91

90
Pair of bowls with
kinrande decoration.
16th century. Diameter
10.2 cm. PDF A464 and
A465

91
Yixing ware cup in the
shape of half a peach
stone. 16th-17th century.
Length 10.1 cm. PDF A84

gold being applied to a white surface (**90**). On the base of these bowls
four characters are written in underglaze blue which read *fugui jiaqi*
(fine vessel for the rich and honourable). The bowls are also unusual in
that the gold decoration is in remarkably good condition.

The Foundation has a small collection of pieces made at the Yixing
kilns in southern Jiangsu province. These kilns specialized in making
stonewares from a local dark clay known as 'purple sand'. A small cup
in the shape of half a peach stone (**91**) was made at these kilns. The
outside of the cup and the rim are both unglazed, but the inside has a
crackled lavender coloured glaze. There are inscriptions incised into the
rim, in two slightly different scripts. One inscription may be translated:
'Xi Wang Mu [The Queen Mother of the West] bestowed the peach
upon the emperor Wu of the Han dynasty'. This refers to the legend that
the tree bearing the peaches of immortality grew in the garden of the
Queen Mother of the West, and that she gave four of them to the Han
emperor Wu when she visited him. Another inscription reads: 'Xuanhe
Hall'; this was a structure built by order of the Song emperor Zhezong
and completed in 1095. A third inscription states that it was 'Recorded
on the cyclical day *ding yu* in the cyclical
month *jia shen* of the cyclical year
geng zi'. The last inscription reads:
'Made by the hand of the Old
Man who loves leisure'. Despite
its claims to antiquity this cup probably dates to the end of the Ming dynasty,
when several potters at Yixing were known
to make copies of Song wares.

The Wares of the Qing Dynasty

1644-1911

With the Qing dynasty China once again came under foreign rule, this time that of the Manchus. They were a tribal people who invaded China from the northwest, making raids south of the Great Wall from 1629 onwards, until the Chinese capital, Beijing, fell to their armies in 1644. Even after the fall of Beijing it was several decades before the Manchus were able to subdue the resistance put up by factions who remained loyal to the Ming dynasty. During the ensuing civil war the southern regions of China suffered badly from being the battlefield of many of the struggles. Among the areas affected was that around the porcelain-producing town of Jingdezhen, which in 1674 was razed to the ground. The situation was so bad that in 1680 the Kangxi emperor ordered an enquiry into the state of the pottery industry; this resulted in the establishment of a well organized kiln complex which by 1683 was able to supply porcelain to the court. There was by this time a system whereby private kilns supplied the general domestic and export market, while officially controlled kilns supplied the court. During the late 17th and 18th century a succession of several very able men held the position of director of the official kilns, and they undoubtedly played a large part in the technological and artistic developments which took place.

One of these kiln directors was Lang Tingji, who held the post from 1705 to 1712. It is he who is credited with producing the fine copper red monochrome glazes that achieved for the first time a depth and brilliance comparable to those of their 15th century prototypes. Copper red monochromes were a particular challenge to the potter since the firing temperature and the kiln atmosphere had to be precisely controlled if the copper was not to volatilize and the brilliant red colour was to be achieved. The Foundation has a particularly comprehensive collection of copper red mono-chromes, as has been noted above in connection with the earlier wares. A large bowl with straight rim and deeply curving base dates to the beginning of the 18th century (**92**). This bowl has the same white rim as the 15th century piece (88) but has a gradation of colour, paler at the top and deepening to a rich crimson towards the base.

92
Large bowl with copper red glaze. *c.* 1700. Diameter 24.2 cm. PDF 513

93
Water pot with incised decoration under 'peach bloom' glaze. Kangxi mark and period (1662-1722). Diameter 12.7 cm. PDF 580

A development of this monochrome copper red glaze was another glaze type that is known in the West as 'peach bloom' but in China as *pingguo hong* (apple red). This was an even more difficult glaze to produce successfully since the desired effect was that of a soft pinkish red with delicate suffusions of green. The glaze seems to have been perfected during the early 18th century, and was

applied to eight specific shapes – all the sort of small items that would have been used on the scholar's desk. An exquisite example of a beehive-shaped water pot (for use when writing or painting with brush and ink) with 'peach bloom' glaze is (**93**). This shape is called a *jizhao zun* in Chinese, which means 'chicken coop jar'. It is essentially a hemisphere with a short neck and slightly everted rim. Under the glaze there is an incised design of three dragon roundels. On the flat base of the vessel is a six-character Kangxi mark in underglaze blue beneath a colourless glaze.

An elongated version of this shape is also found among the monochrome wares of the Kangxi period. An example is the water pot with transparent celadon-like glaze on a porcelain body (**94**). This pot has a graceful design of floating clouds carved and incised into the body under the glaze. On the flat white base a six-character Kangxi mark has been written in underglaze blue.

94
Water pot with carved and incised decoration under a celadon-type glaze. Kangxi mark and period (1662-1722). Height 7.7 cm. PDF 583

As has already been noted, the David Foundation also has a comprehensive collection of monochrome yellow wares. Among these is an impressive *guan* jar, which has managed to retain its domed lid with knob shaped like a lotus bud (**95**)

95
Jar and cover with yellow enamel over the glaze. Kangxi mark and period (1662-1722). Height 26.7cm. PDF A527

It is just possible to see that the jar was thrown in two parts and then luted together at the point where a fine ridge is visible around the body of the vessel. This piece also has an underglaze blue Kangxi mark on the base. One of the most skilfully decorated of the yellow glazed wares is a small table screen (96), which has a design applied in relief under the glaze. The choice of mo-

96
Table screen with relief decoration under yellow enamel overglaze. First half of 18th century. Height 23.5 cm. PDF 539

tif is a cock and cockscomb plant, which provide a pun in Chinese for 'one official hat on top of another', to encourage the scholar-official on whose desk it stood to strive for greater advancement within the Chinese civil service.

During the reign of the Yongzheng emperor considerable experimentation took place with new glaze colours, and a range of delicately potted wares with a wide variety of new colours was produced. Among the wares that were given to the Foundation by the Honourable Mountstuart Elphinstone are some examples of these new colours. The bright citrus yellow glaze on the moulded dish in the shape of an open lotus flower with the seed pod in the centre (97) is quite different from the warm yellow glazes mentioned above. The small elongated ovoid vase has an opaque rose coloured glaze. The little hemispherical bowl is one of a pair which have a plain white inside and an opaque lime green applied over the outside. On another little bowl is a very pale and delicate cobalt blue glaze. The pale blue, green and yellow pieces have a blue underglaze Yongzheng mark written under the colourless glaze on their bases. The rose vase has a Yongzheng mark in seal script impressed into its base. The pale matt turquoise glazed vase with pear-shaped body and long tubular neck probably also dates to the same

97
Group of monochrome porcelains.
Yellow dish: Yongzheng mark and period. Diameter 29.5 cm. PDF B538
Turquoise vase: first half of 18th century. Height 19.1 cm. PDF B535
Rose vase: Yongzheng mark and period. Height 14.6 cm. PDF B53
Blue bowl: Yongzheng mark and period. Diameter 14.6 cm. PDF B557
Green bowl: Yongzheng mark and period (1723-35). Diameter 10.2 cm. PDF B524
Black box: Kangxi period (1662-1722). Diameter 10.2 cm. PDF B547

period. The round black box bears a Kangxi mark on its base. This box has the dense black glaze that was also used on archaistic shapes later in the century. This piece was once decorated with a design of gilded dragons, but, like the majority of the *kinrande* wares of the 16th century, the gilding has largely rubbed off.

The fashion for archaistic wares reached its peak during the reign of the Qianlong emperor, and it is to this period that the two turquoise vases (**98**) almost certainly belong. Unlike that of the small pale turquoise vase seen in the previous plate, the glaze on these vases is transparent and jewel-like. They have been made in the shape of ancient bronze *gu* wine vessels, and even the decoration under the glaze has been adapted from that on the original bronzes. Around the thickened central band there is a debased archaic dragon design.

It is not possible to leave the monochrome wares without mentioning the exceptional collection of white porcelains from the Dehua kilns in Fujian province. Many of the examples of this type of porcelain that found their way to the West are of rather poor quality, and so it is particularly fortunate that this group of finely made pieces in the David Foundation is available for study. A number of the figures are master-pieces of the potter's skill, and none more so than the seated figure of the Bodhisattva Guanyin, who came to be regarded as the Goddess of Mercy (**99**). Not only are the folds of her garments beautifully modelled, but elements such as her fingers and the fish in her basket are also modelled with remarkable delicacy. On the back of the figure a four-character seal mark has been impressed into the porcelain under the glaze. This appears to be the seal of the potter He Chaozong, who worked in the second half of the 17th century. Usually the Chinese potter is anonymous, but at the kilns of Dehua and Yixing, individual potters or families of potters frequently applied their seals to their pieces, while occasionally Cizhou potters would inscribe their wares with their family name.

Notwithstanding the difficulties besetting Jingde-zhen during the last reigns of the Ming and the first decades of the Qing dynasty, the wares decorated in underglaze blue produced there during the so-called 'transitional period' (1620-80) do include some well made and

98
Pair of vases with turquoise glaze over moulded decoration. Qianlong period (1736-95). Height 27.9 cm. PDF B588 and B589

99
Dehua figure of the Bodhisattva Guanyin. Late 17th century. Height 14 cm. PDF 415

100
Basin with underglaze
blue decoration. 1640s.
Diameter 19.1 cm.
PDF 613

interesting pieces. Among the finest of these is the basin with swelling sides (**100**). As is typical of pieces of the Chongzhen period, the basin has a decorative band incised into the body material under the glaze just below the mouthrim, but is otherwise free of minor bands of decoration. The main decorative area has ample white space around it. This area is finely painted with a scene depicting the corpulent form of Budai Heshang (the fat Buddha associated with good fortune) seated under a tree, apparently dozing while children play around him. The accomplished painting of the tree and the scudding clouds, as well as of the grass in v-shaped clumps, is characteristic of these wares. This basin probably dates to the 1640s.

One of the features that is most noticeable in the porcelains of the Kangxi, Yongzheng and Qianlong periods is the complete technical mastery achieved by the potters at Jingdezhen. This mastery is admirably demonstrated on a vase with narrow shoulders and a wide neck decorated with a design of dragons, rocks, waves and clouds in low carved relief (**101**). The design itself is a powerful one, but it is the superb control that the potter has exercised over the cobalt blue and more especially over the copper red and green that is particularly impressive, in combination with the celadon-like glaze that has been used on the

101
Vase with underglaze
blue and red decoration.
Kangxi mark and period
(1662-1722). Height
42 cm. PDF C644

rocks. The dragon is painted in copper red with close attention to detail, but certain elements, most noticeably the creature's head, have been treated like that on the 'peach bloom' glazed ware (93) and patches of green have been allowed to break through the red. The base of the vase bears a Kangxi mark in underglaze blue inside a double ring.

The precision of the painting in cobalt blue is even more marked on the wares dating to the Qianlong period. This precision is to be found on those underglaze blue decorated wares inspired by ancient bronze vessels. It is also to be seen on those blue and white pieces that aim to imitate the wares of the 15th century. One such piece is the bowl (**102**), which

102
Bowl with underglaze blue decoration. Qianlong mark and period (1736-95). Diameter 21.3 cm. PDF B673

is a direct copy of a 15th century bowl bearing a Xuande mark in the David Collection (PDF B636). The Qianlong bowl has slightly rounded sides and a flared rim. It is finely potted and stands on a straight foot. On the inside of the bowl there is a design of floral scrolls in white slip under the glaze and an underglaze blue flower medallion in the centre, while around the outside is a lotus scroll and just above the foot a band of overlapping petals. The decorative scheme on this bowl precisely mirrors that on the 15th century bowl, but the overall effect is changed in a number of ways. First, the Qianlong bowl is more finely potted than the earlier example. Second, the glaze on the 18th century bowl is very glossy and completely colourless instead of having the slight greenish tinge of the 15th century wares. Third, the cobalt blue is painted on with such precision that the fluency of the original is lost, and even the attempt to create artificially the 'heaped and piled' effect of the early 15th century has resulted in a rather mannered style.

We have already noted this copying of 15th century styles in the 18th century in the case of the *doucai* 'chicken cups' (79). Although a number of the pieces that were produced after the reawakening of interest in *doucai* wares in the 18th century did model themselves on (or in cases like that of the 'chicken cups' set out to copy directly) the 15th century wares, a new style was also developed. This new style was characterized by the same delicacy seen on the new types of overglaze

103

Teapot with *doucai* decoration. Yongzheng mark and period (1723-35). Height 13.8 cm. PDF A798

enamelled wares developed at this time, which will be discussed below. The 18th century *doucai* style is epitomized by the teapot (**103**). The vessel has an ovoid body and the spout and handle are simply curved. The decorative motif is the familiar 'three friends of winter' – pine, bamboo and prunus – which have soft underglaze blue outlines. The overglaze colours have been applied, in the case of the green and aubergine as pale washes, but the design has been punctuated by carefully placed tiny bright red splashes indicating the prunus flowers. There are no minor decorative bands employed in this style of decoration. A six-character mark of Yongzheng appears in underglaze blue on the base.

A development of the earlier *wucai* style is to be seen in a set of twelve wine cups dating to the Kangxi period (**104**). These cups are made of fine 'eggshell' porcelain, and combine elements of underglaze blue with delicate painting in overglaze enamels using the *famille verte* palette. They are beautifully painted, each cup being decorated with one of the flowers of the twelve months, and with an appropriate poetic inscription in underglaze blue on the back. On the fifth month cup, for

104

Set of twelve cups with *wucai* decoration. Kangxi mark and period (1662-1722). Height 6.5 cm. PDF 815 a-l

instance, there is a painting of crab-apple on one side and a poem on the other which may be translated:

The fragrance combines with the scent of the nocturnal rain,
Their beautiful colours stand out in sunshine or mist.

It is rare to find a complete set of these Kangxi cups, which were frequently copied in the succeeding reign periods, and they are shown in order starting from the top left. The first month is represented by prunus, followed by magnolia or wintersweet, peach, rose, crab-apple, peony, lotus, pomegranate, tall mallow, chrysanthemum, orchid and narcissus. It should be noted, however, that the choice of flowers for the twelve months does vary slightly between different decorative schemes. On these pieces, the underglaze blue elements in the design are mainly confined to the ground or rocks, but there are some exceptions. In the cup third from the right in the upper row, for example, the underglaze blue has been combined with overglaze black to paint the persimmon fruit in a style that is very reminiscent of the famous painting, *Six Persimmons*, by the 13th century Chan Buddhist artist Mu Qi.

105
Bowl with overglaze enamel decoration. Early 18th century. Diameter 22.5 cm. PDF 859

The change in painting style that can be seen on the twelve cups is typical of the changes that occurred in the late 17th and early 18th century on fine wares decorated with overglaze enamels. Due to technological innovations in glazes and enamels it became possible for the ceramic decorators to produce overglaze painting of a delicacy and clarity that had not previously been possible. The two categories of enamelled wares that are best known in the West are *famille verte* and *famille rose*. These names were coined by Jacquemart and Le Blant in their book on the history of porcelain published in Paris in 1862. They are not terms used by the Chinese themselves but are nevertheless both useful and descriptive. The *famille verte* palette takes its name from the variety of transparent greens that are included in it. This is, indeed, basically a transparent palette including aubergine, yellow, and a newly developed cobalt blue overglaze enamel. The two colours that are not transparent are the iron red and the black. In the case of the black this had, in the early stages, to be covered with a clear pale green enamel in order to give it an appropriately lustrous appearance. Small amounts of gilding are also used.

One of a pair of bowls in the David Foundation (**105**) displays all the fine points of these *famille verte* porcelains. The main decorative band is painted with rocks and Daoist fairies accompanied by various symbols of longevity. The Daoist fairies are in two groups, and the figure leading both the groups is probably Xi Wang Mu (The Queen Mother of the West) who is carrying a *ruyi* sceptre. The first group is following a chariot that is filled with peaches and *lingzhi* fungus, both symbols of longevity. This chariot is being pulled by a disgruntled-looking wolf, and following the procession is a spotted deer, which along with the crane is a familiar of Shou Lao (the Star God of Longevity), hence also a symbol of long life. In the second group Xi Wang Mu is accompanied by a crane. She is depicted riding on this crane on the other bowl of the pair. The figures that make up the group carry baskets filled with peaches and *lingzhi* fungus. One of them holds a double gourd flask from which emanate five red bats, symbolizing the Five Blessings (longevity, riches, health, love of virtue, and a good end crowning the life). In Chinese the word for bat – *fu* – sounds the same as the word for happiness (although they are written differently), and thus the bat is taken as a symbol of happiness. Since red is regarded as an auspicious colour, red bats are particularly favoured. Around the foot of the bowl is a design of butterflies, flower sprays and single petals.

This same design is to be seen around the small dish (**106, right**).

106
Dishes with overglaze enamel decoration. Both with Chenghua marks but dating to the early 18th century. Diameters 20.3 cm and 17.2 cm. PDF 803 and 808

107
Dish with overglaze
enamel decoration.
Kangxi mark and period
(1662-1722). Diameter
25.1 cm. PDF A836

This is one of several such plates in the David Collection decorated in this style and bearing a six-character mark of Chenghua in underglaze blue on the base although the piece in fact dates to the early 18th century. This dish is decorated with graceful figures painted in the same way as the ones on the previous bowl, with the faces outlined in red enamel. The garments of these figures are painted in as much detail as is possible when using a palette that does not allow blending of colours. The texture of the ground and the rocks is achieved by applying black brush strokes under a green enamel. The rocks behind the figures also show the use of juxtaposed blocks of colour to create an impression of mass.

The other dish with a Chenghua reign mark on its base (**106, left**), also dates to the early 18th century. The style of this dish is, however, slightly different, being closer in some ways to that seen on paintings. The choice of subject is also one that is very popular among artists – that of a scholar seated on a rock beneath a pine tree. In this case the scholar is intently watching a fight between two roosters. The central design, with distracting details kept to a minimum, is restricted to the flat base area. The overglaze enamels used include the new cobalt blue.

The Foundation has four examples of a particular group of plates decorated in *famille verte* enamels. They are of similar shape, all having rounded sides and flat rims, and like the one illustrated (**107**) , they are

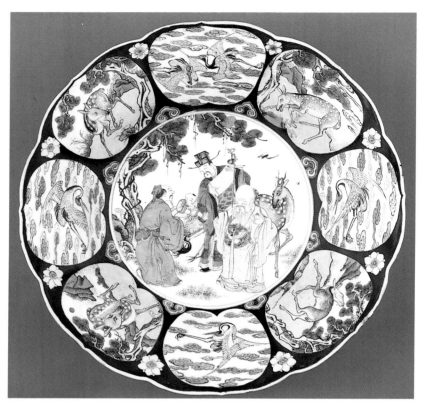

decorated in a very finely painted style. Around the edge of the plate is a decorative band that looks rather like brocade and has been painted in iron red enamel. There are four medallions inset at regular intervals within the brocade border. Each of these medallions contains a Chinese character written in a type of seal script. The characters read *wan shou wu jiang* (ten thousand years of long life without end). This is the traditional imperial birthday greeting, and it is thought that these plates may have been made for the sixtieth birthday of the emperor Kangxi in 1713.

108
Dish with overglaze enamel decoration. Chenghua mark but dating to the late 17th century. Diameter 34.7 cm. PDF A821

Like several other pieces discussed above this plate has a design of ducks swimming on a lotus pond. This is very delicately painted with considerable attention to detail, even to the extent of showing the ragged holes at the edges of the browning lotus leaves.

One of the subgroups of the *famille verte* palette is that known as *famille noire*. The name derives from the dense black background that is applied around reserved areas of *famille verte* painting. A fine example of *famille noire* decoration is the dish illustrated (**108**). Like the two dishes (106), it has a Chenghua mark written in underglaze blue on its base. It actually dates to the late 17th century, and is a particularly early example of the use of overglaze blue enamel, and includes some gilding. Around the slightly foliated and everted rim are eight reserved leaf-shaped panels alternately decorated with spotted deer in landscape under pine trees and with cranes amongst multicoloured clouds. Individual white flowers and green and yellow *ruyi* heads have been placed between the panels top and bottom. The central area has been painted with a group consisting of the Three Star Gods of Happiness, Rank and Longevity, who are generally regarded as the Triad of the Daoist pantheon. They are accompanied by a small boy, a crane and a spotted deer, and stand under a gnarled pine tree, through the branches of which a red sun can be seen. On the back of the dish a design of bamboo sprays has been painted in sepia enamel.

The use of this sepia enamel to imitate the effect of ink painting on silk or paper became quite popular around the middle of the 18th century, and two dishes in the Foundation demonstrate just how successfully landscape paintings could be reproduced on porcelain (**109**). Many Chinese painters often eschew colour in favour of the tonal qualities of black ink, especially for landscape paintings. One of these was the Yuan dynasty artist Ni Zan, the influence of whose works can be seen on the two dishes. As in some of Ni Zan's paintings, tiny touches of red have been used in the predominantly black and white landscape. On one bowl is a red sun, and on the other the sun, a small pavilion and the fisherman's coat are all red. Perhaps the most remarkable thing about these dishes is that the viewer is not aware that the landscapes have been painted on a curved surface, so well has the ceramic artist compensated for the curvature. This is something that the Chinese porcelain painter does with consummate skill. On the base of these bowls is written *Yayu tang zhi* (Made for the Hall of Elegant Rain). Yayu tang was the hall-name of the scholar-official Lu Jianzeng (1690-1768).

The last major development in overglaze enamelled porcelains was that of the *famille rose* palette. The name derives from a rose pink enamel that was made using colloidal gold, but two other colours were

109
Pair of dishes with overglaze enamel decoration. Mid 18th century. Diameter 20 cm. PDF 842

added to the range available in the *famille verte* palette: opaque yellow and opaque white. Of these three new colours it is the white that is really the most significant in changing the style of painting, as it could be combined with other colours to produce blended and pastel colours. A 'precious moon flask' in Sir Percival's collection has a design that uses the new enamels to the full (**110**). On one side of the flask richly coloured birds sit among the branches of pink and white rose-peonies. The stamens of the flowers have been painted in opaque enamel, the impasto quality of which has been fully utilized in order to achieve a slight relief effect. The mixing and shading qualities of the pink and the white enamels have been exploited to the utmost, and especially on the white blossoms where the effect is very delicate. The outlines of the pink flowers have been drawn in fine iron red lines. On the other side of the flask two delicately drawn white birds are shown among the branches of a blossoming peach tree. There are also blue chrysanthemum flowers and fluttering butterflies. On the base of the flask there is an underglaze blue mark of Yongzheng written in seal script.

110
Flask with overglaze enamel decoration. Yongzheng mark and period (1723-35). Height 29.3 cm. PDF 824

The large dish (**111**) provides further evidence of the versatility of these *famille rose* enamels. On the flowers of the tree peony and prunus there is subtle blending of white, pink and green enamel. The peaches have been painted so as to reproduce their texture by means of a mixture of blending and stippling. This dish also displays a decorative device, seen on a number of pieces of this period, whereby the composition begins on the outside and continues over the edge of the dish and onto the inside where the major area of the decoration is found. A further indication that the decoration of inside and outside are supposed to be 'read' together is

the fact that there are two red bats on the inside of the dish and three on the outside, making up the five red bats symbolizing the Five Blessings.

Two of the most exquisitely painted pieces among these *famille rose* porcelains are the teapot and cup (**112**). Both are decorated with a design of lotus blossoms and leaves. As well as being one of the flowers of the twelve months, the lotus is also associated with Buddhism and with the idea of purity, since the lovely flowers arise unsullied from the mud. A feature of *famille rose* decoration that has not so far been mentioned is well illustrated by these pieces. The painting of the flowers

111
Large dish with overglaze enamel decoration. Yongzheng mark and period (1723-35). Diameter 50.8 cm. PDF A840

112
Teapot and cup with over-
glaze enamel decoration.
Yongzheng mark and
period (1723-35).
Teapot: Height 11.1 cm.
Cup: Diameter 6.3 cm.
PDF A825 and A826

makes full use of the blending characteristics of the opaque colours, and two methods of outlining the flowers are employed: either a fine dark enamel line is painted around the pale flowers, or a narrow white band is reserved around the pink petals. The greens used for the leaves and stems, however, are still the transparent colours of the *famille verte* palette which could not be blended, or indeed reserved as they tended to spread very slightly when fired. Instead the juxtaposition of blocks of colour continued to be used, and texture and outlines were added using black enamel. On the back of both pieces there is a poetic inscription which may be translated:

Pure as the virtue of the superior man,
Elegant as the maquillage of a great beauty.

Both pieces also bear three red seals, one of which is common to both pieces. On the base of both teapot and cup there is a four-character mark of Yongzheng written in overglaze blue enamel.

On the ovoid vase (**113**) can be seen the effect of European painting on the Chinese ceramic decorator. There were a number of European Jesuit missionary artists working at the Chinese court in the 18th century. The most famous of these was Giuseppe Castiglione, who was known in China as Lang Shining. The Western artists had a considerable impact not least in the introduction of European ideas of perspective and shading. Nian Xiyao, who was director of the imperial kilns from 1726, claimed in his treatise on draughtsmanship that he had been taught by Castiglione. The shepherdess on this vase, though clad in Chinese dress, is nevertheless a Western motif. Her face has been shaded very delicately, and the folds of her garments are emphasized by techniques of shading that had previously been unknown in China. A frivolous but charming use of the impasto quality of the white enamel can be seen on the fleece of the three sheep. Each curl has been rendered in very slight relief, and then has been outlined in sepia enamel. The two seal characters to the left of the figure read 'seal of Chen' and may be the name of the decorator. This vase dates to the second quarter of the 18th century.

113
Vase with overglaze
enamel decoration.
Second quarter of 18th
century. Height 31.5 cm.
PDF 881

Finally some decorated wares that are not made of porcelain should be mentioned. Sir Percival also acquired a small group of very finely painted glass items, which bear a close resemblance to some of the fine enamelled porcelains; three of these glass pieces are shown in (**114**). On the cylindrical brush barrel the decoration includes the Seven Sages. Three of them are sitting listening to a fourth who is seated on a rock under a pine tree, while another figure in the background stands looking on. On the other side of the vessel a young man is shown presenting peaches to a bearded figure holding a twisted staff. The faces of the figures have been shaded and they appear in a landscape setting complete with blue sky. On the base of the brush barrel a four-character mark of Qianlong has been incised and then filled with blue enamel. The little vase is painted in a style very similar to that seen on some porcelain examples in the Collection. Around the base is a scrolling band painted in pink, while the main decorative area has a design of flowering pink and yellow peonies with rocks and blue chrysanthemums. On the

114
Group of glass vessels
with enamel decoration.
All have Qianlong marks
and are of the period
(1736-95).
Brush pot: Height 10.1 cm.
PDF 854
Vase: Height 9.1 cm.
PDF 852
Cup: Height 4.3 cm.
PDF 850

back a poetic inscription has been painted in black enamel with three red
seals. The inscription may be translated:

Its tender buds enclose golden pollen;
Its heavy flowers form embroidered bags.

On the base of this piece too there is an incised four-character mark of
Qianlong filled with blue enamel.

The tiny cup to the right of the vase bears the same mark on its base,
and it has been decorated with an exceptionally finely painted design
of panels depicting summer and winter landscapes set within decorative scrolls and flowers. Around its footring is a scrolling band. As on the
last porcelain vase, the influence of European painting styles can be
clearly seen in the decoration on both the brush pot and the cup.

While this guide to the Collection cannot present a comprehensive view
of the wares in the Percival David Foundation, it is hoped that the fore-
going may serve as an introduction to the main areas of the Collection
and provide a brief survey of the developments in Chinese ceramics
against which the pieces may be seen. A selected bibliography is
provided below for the benefit of those readers who would like further
information on the ceramics in the Foundation.

Selected Bibliography

David, Lady, *Illustrated Catalogue of Ch'ing Enamelled Ware in the Percival David Foundation of Chinese Art*, London, 1973

David, Sir Percival, 'Some Notes on Pi-se Yao', *Eastern Art*, Vol. 1, No. 3, January 1929, pp. 137-43

David, Sir Percival, 'A Commentary on Ju Ware', *Transactions of the Oriental Ceramic Society*, 1936-37, pp. 18-69

David, Sir Percival, *Chinese Connoisseurship: The Ko Ku Yao Lun, The Essential Criteria of Antiquities*, London, 1971

Hobson, R.L., *A Catalogue of Chinese Pottery and Porcelain in the Collection of Sir Percival David, Bt., F.S.A.*, London, 1934

Kerr, Rose, *Chinese Ceramics, Porcelain of the Qing Dynasty 1644-1911*, Victoria and Albert Museum, London, 1986

Kerr, Rose, 'Yuan and Ming Porcelains in the Percival David Foundation of Chinese Art', *Arts of Asia*, January-February 1989, pp. 90-8

Krahl, Regina, *Chinese Ceramics in the Topkapi Saray Museum Istanbul*, Vol. II, London, 1986

Lion-Goldschmidt, Daisy, *Ming Porcelain,* Thames and Hudson, London, 1978

Medley, Margaret, *Illustrated Catalogue of Ming and Ch'ing Monochrome in the Percival David Foundation of Chinese Art*, London, 1973

Medley, Margaret, *Illustrated Catalogue of Underglaze Blue and Copper Red Decorated Porcelains*, Percival David Foundation of Chinese Art, London, 1976

Medley, Margaret, *Illustrated Catalogue of Celadon Wares*, Percival David Foundation of Chinese Art, London, 1977

Medley, Margaret, *Illustrated Catalogue of Ming Polychrome Wares*, Percival David Foundation of Chinese Art, London, 1978

Medley, Margaret, *Illustrated Catalogue of Ting and Allied Wares*, Percival David Foundation of Chinese Art, London, 1980

Pope, John A., *Chinese Porcelains from the Ardebil Shrine* (2nd ed.), London, 1981

Riddell, Sheila, *Dated Chinese Antiquities 600-1650*, London, 1979

Scott, Rosemary E., 'A Great Connoisseur', *The Antique Collector*, 3, 1986, pp. 64-9

Scott, Rosemary E., 'Fine Porcelain and Delicate Brushwork – A Group of Qing Dynasty Wares with Overglaze Enamel Decoration from the Percival David Foundation', *Orientations*, November 1986, pp. 22-35

Scott, Rosemary E., '18th century overglaze enamels: the influence of technological development on painting style', *Style in the East Asian Tradition* (eds. Scott, R. & Hutt, G.), London, 1987, pp. 149-68

Scott, Rosemary E., 'Early Monochrome Wares in the Percival David Foundation', *Arts of Asia*, January-February 1989, pp. 77-89

Scott, Rosemary E., 'Ch'ing Porcelains in the Percival David Foundation', *Arts of Asia*, January-February 1989, pp. 99-111

Scott, Rosemary E., 'Some influences on the painting styles of Qing overglaze enamel wares', *Imperial Taste – Chinese Ceramics from the Percival David Foundation*, Chronicle Books, San Francisco, 1989

Tregear, Mary, *Song Ceramics*, Thames and Hudson, London, 1982

Wang Qingzheng, Fan Dongqing and Zhou Lili, *The Discovery of the Ru Kiln*, Hong Kong, 1987

Wang Qingzheng (ed.), *Underglaze Blue and Red*, Hong Kong, 1987

Ye Zhemin, 'A Report on Investigation of the Ru Kiln for 20 Years', *Zhongguo taoci*, 1987, no. 6, pp. 41-6

Yorke Hardy, S., *Illustrated Catalogue of Tung, Ju, Kuan, Chün, Kuang-Tung & Glazed I-Hsing Wares in the Percival David Foundation of Chinese Art*, London, 1953

York Hardy, Sheila, 'Ku Yüeh Hsüan – A New Hypothesis', *Oriental Art*, II (1949), No. 3, pp. 116-25